This ambitious study argues that our modern conception of the aesthetic sphere emerged during the era of British and German Romanticism from conflicts between competing models of the liberal state and the cultural nation. The aesthetic sphere is thus centrally connected to "aesthetic statism," which is the theoretical project of reconciling conflicts in the political sphere by appealing to the unity of the symbol. David Kaiser traces the trajectory of aesthetic statism from Schiller and Coleridge, through Arnold, Mill, and Ruskin, to Adorno and Habermas. He analyzes how the concept of aesthetic autonomy shifts from being a supplement to the political sphere to an end in itself; this shift lies behind the problems that contemporary literary theory has faced in its attempts to connect the aesthetic and political spheres. Finally, he suggests that we rethink the aesthetic sphere in order to regain that connection.

DAVID ARAM KAISER gained his Ph.D. from the University of California, Berkeley, and has taught at the University of Kentucky. He has published articles in, amongst other journals, *Studies in Romanticism* and *European Romantic Review*.

CAMBRIDGE STUDIES IN ROMANTICISM 34

ROMANTICISM, AESTHETICS, AND NATIONALISM

CAMBRIDGE STUDIES IN ROMANTICISM 34

General editors
Professor Marilyn Butler
University of Oxford
Professor James Chandler
University of Chicago

Editorial board
John Barrell, *University of York*
Paul Hamilton, *University of London*
Mary Jacobus, *Cornell University*
Kenneth Johnston, *Indiana University*
Alan Liu, *University of California, Santa Barbara*
Jerome McGann, *University of Virginia*
David Simpson, *University of California*

This series aims to foster the best new work in one of the most challenging fields within English literary studies. From the early 1780s to the early 1830s a formidable array of talented men and women took to literary composition, not just in poetry, which some of them famously transformed, but in many modes of writing. The expansion of publishing created new opportunities for writers, and the political stakes of what they wrote were raised again by what Wordsworth called those "great national events" that were "almost daily taking place": the French Revolution, the Napoleonic and American wars, urbanization, industrialization, religious revival, an expanded empire abroad, and the reform movement at home. This was an enormous ambition, even when it pretended otherwise. The relations between science, philosophy, religion, and literature were reworked in texts such as *Frankenstein* and *Biographia Literaria*; gender relations in *A Vindication of the Rights of Woman* and *Don Juan*; journalism by Cobbett and Hazlitt; poetic form, content, and style by the Lake School and the Cockney School. Outside Shakespeare studies, probably no body of writing has produced such a wealth of responses of modern criticism. This indeed is the period that saw the emergence of those notions of "literature" and of literary history, especially national literary history, on which modern scholarship in English has been founded.

The categories produced by Romanticism have also been challenged by recent historicist arguments. The task of the series is to engage both with a challenging corpus of Romantic writings and with the changing field of criticism they have helped to shape. As with other literary series published by Cambridge, this one will represent the work of both younger and more established scholars, on either side of the Atlantic and elsewhere.

For a complete list of titles published see end of book

ROMANTICISM, AESTHETICS, AND NATIONALISM

DAVID ARAM KAISER

CAMBRIDGE UNIVERSITY PRESS

PUBLISHED BY THE PRESS SYNDICATE OF THE UNIVERSITY OF CAMBRIDGE
The Pitt Building, Trumpington Street, Cambridge, United Kingdom

CAMBRIDGE UNIVERSITY PRESS
The Edinburgh Building, Cambridge CB2 2RU, UK   http://www.cup.cam.ac.uk
40 West 20th Street, New York, NY 10011-4211, USA   http://www.cup.org
10 Stamford Road, Oakleigh, Melbourne 3166, Australia

© David Aram Kaiser 1999

This book is in copyright. Subject to statutory exception and to the provisions of
relevant collective licensing agreements, no reproduction of any part may take place
without the written permission of Cambridge University Press.

First published 1999

Printed in the United Kingdom at the University Press, Cambridge

Typeset in Baskerville 11/12.5pt [VN]

A catalogue record for this book is available from the British Library

Library of Congress cataloguing in publication data
Kaiser, David Aram.
Romanticism, aesthetics, and nationalism / David Aram Kaiser.
p.   cm. – (Cambridge Studies in Romanticism; 34)
ISBN 0 521 63000 2
1. Literature – History and criticism.   2. Aesthetics, Modern.   3. Romanticism.
4. Nationalism in literature.   5. Politics and literature.   I. Title.   II. Series.
PN49.K2512   1999
801'.93 – dc21   99-11997   CIP

ISBN 0 521 63000 2 hardback

This book is dedicated to my parents, Frank Charles and Nectar Zailian Kaiser, without whose spiritual and material support this book could never have been written. Their belief in the fundamental value and power of culture was a central formative influence on me. I consider it a gift I freely accepted, and for this too I am very grateful.

Contents

Acknowledgements	*page* xi
List of abbreviations	xii

	Introduction	1
1	Modernity, subjectivity, liberalism, and nationalism	11
2	The symbol and the aesthetic sphere	28
3	Schiller's aesthetic state	39
4	Symbol, state, and Clerisy: the aesthetic politics of Coleridge	59
5	The best self and the private self: Matthew Arnold on culture and the state	74
6	Aesthetic kingship and queenship: Ruskin on the state and the home	92
7	The aesthetic and political spheres in contemporary theory: Adorno and Habermas	111

Notes	137
Index	152

Acknowledgements

Parts of chapter 2 first appeared in a different form in "The Incarnated Symbol: Coleridge, Hegel, Strauss, and the Higher Biblical Criticism," *European Romantic Review*, vol. 4, no. 2, Winter 1994, 133–50.

Parts of chapter 3 first appeared in a different form in "Whither Kantian Aesthetics?," *Eighteenth-Century Life*, vol. 20, no. 1, February 1996, 101–08.

Parts of chapter 4 first appeared in a different form in "'The Perfection of Reason': Coleridge and the Ancient Constitution," *Studies in Romanticism*, vol. 32, no. 1, Spring 1993, 29–55.

I am grateful to the editors of these journals for the permission to use these materials.

I would like to acknowledge the following individuals: Joseph Tussman, who first presented to me the idea that the political could be rational. David Lloyd, who opened up for me British Marxist cultural studies and the Frankfurt school. The American pragmatists, Walter Benn Michaels, Stanley Fish, and Steven Knapp, with whom I argued constantly, but, I hope, ultimately beneficially. Hans Sluga, for explorations of the German philosophical tradition. The members of the University of Kentucky's Committee for Social Theory, for providing a comradely interdisciplinary forum for discussion and exploration of critical theory. Jim Wilkinson, for lengthy discussions of all things Hegelian. Adam Potkay, Michael Moon, and Dana Nelson for their sound professional advice at various points of this project. Jürgen Habermas, for directing me to central texts about aesthetic issues within the vast literature by and about him. The two readers for Cambridge University Press, especially the first for numerous detailed suggestions for revision. James Chandler, for a penetrating reading of the penultimate version of the manuscript which helped in making the push of final revision. Finally, my wife Jo Ellen Green Kaiser, whose presence and partnership, from first discussions to final editing, helped make this book possible.

Abbreviations

AL   Friedrich Schiller, *On the Aesthetic Education of Man, in a Series of Letters*, trans. Elizabeth Wilkinson and L. A. Willoughby, (Oxford: Clarendon Press, 1967). Quotations will be identified in the text by letter number in roman and paragraph number in arabic numerals.

AT   Theodor W. Adorno, *Aesthetic Theory*, trans. Robert Hullot-Kentor (Minneapolis: University of Minnesota Press, 1997)

C&A   Matthew Arnold, *Culture and Anarchy*, ed. Samuel Lipman (New Haven: Yale University Press, 1994)

C&S   Samuel Taylor Coleridge, *On the Constitution of the Church and State, The Collected Works of Samuel Taylor Coleridge*, volume x, ed. John Colmer (Princeton University Press, 1976)

"D"   Matthew Arnold, "Democracy," in *The Complete Prose Works of Matthew Arnold*, volume II, *Democratic Education* (Ann Arbor: University of Michigan Press, 1962)

DE   Max Horkheimer and Theodor W. Adorno, *Dialectic of Enlightenment*, trans. John Cumming (New York: Continuum, 1986)

F   Samuel Taylor Coleridge, *The Friend*, volume I, reprinted in *The Collected Works of Samuel Taylor Coleridge*, volume IV, ed. Barbara Rook (Princeton University Press, 1969)

PD   Jürgen Habermas, *Philosophical Discourse of Modernity*, trans. Frederick Lawrence (Cambridge, Mass.: MIT Press, 1987)

RG   John Stuart Mill, *Considerations on Representative Government*, in *The Collected Works of John Stuart Mill*, volume XIX, *Essays on Politics and Society* (University of Toronto Press, 1977)

SM   Samuel Taylor Coleridge, *The Statesman's Manual*, in *The Collected Works of Samuel Taylor Coleridge*, volume VI, *Lay Sermons*, ed. R. J. White (Princeton University Press, 1972)

"SP"   Matthew Arnold, "The Study of Poetry," in *The Complete Prose Works of Matthew Arnold*, volume IX: *English Literature and Irish Politics* (Ann Arbor: University of Michigan Press, 1973)
ST   Jürgen Habermas, *The Structural Transformation of the Public Sphere: An Inquiry into a Category of Bourgeois Society*, translated by Thomas Burger with the assistance of Frederick Lawrence (Cambridge, Mass.: MIT Press, 1989)
TCA   Jürgen Habermas, *The Theory of Communicative Action*, volume I, *Reason and the Rationalization of Society*, trans. Thomas McCarthy (Boston: Beacon Press, 1984)
"TSR"   Albrect Wellmer, "Truth, Semblance, Reconciliation," in *The Persistence of Modernity*, trans. David Midgley (Cambridge, Mass.: MIT Press, 1991)
WR   John Ruskin, *The Complete Works of John Ruskin*, Library Edition, 39 volumes, ed. E. T. Cook and Alexander Wedderburn (London: George Allen, 1903–12). Quotations will be identified in the text by the volume number followed by the page number.

Introduction

THE PROBLEM OF AESTHETIC INDETERMINACY

In contemporary literary theory, the indeterminate quality of literary language is often connected to progressive political principles, while determinate language is connected to *totalizing* political ideology. It is on this basis, for example, that Jerome McGann values Coleridge's writings over Hegel's:

> Coleridge's theory of Romanticism is the archetypical Romantic theory – brilliant, argumentative, ceaseless, exploratory, incomplete, and not always very clear. Hegel's theory, speculative and total, represents the transformation of Romanticism into acculturated forms, into state ideology. Hegel sentimentalizes Romanticism by domesticating its essential tensions, conflicts, and patterns of internal contradiction.[1]

In this model of literary history, literary indeterminacy both originates in Romanticism and is its archetypal achievement. Because Romanticism has given us indeterminacy, the argument goes, it has also given us the tools of progressive political thought, or, at least, has given us the tools to resist totalizing systems of discourse.

Of the many works of Romanticism associated with the concept of indeterminacy, Schiller's theory of aesthetic *play* in the *Aesthetic Letters* in particular has been viewed as a model of how indeterminacy acts as a force for progressive political development. The contemporary philosopher Richard Rorty, for example, expresses this view when he argues that the value of Schiller's concept of the aesthetic sphere is that it allows one to view political issues as one would aesthetic works rather than as moral imperatives: "I should argue that in the recent history of liberal societies, the willingness to view matters aesthetically – to be content to indulge in what Schiller called 'play' and to discard what Nietzsche called 'the spirit of seriousness' – has been an important vehicle of moral progress."[2] Rorty's account of aesthetic detachment reflects the way that Schiller's account of the concept of aesthetic "play" is typically understood as promoting political progress indirectly, by allowing the individual to occupy a detached position from the political world. According to this view, the value of the aesthetic sphere is that it gives individuals a place to develop their private moral sense by sheltering them from the demands of the public world.

But this typical view of Schiller represents a reversal of Schiller's project in the *Aesthetic Letters*. As I will argue, Schiller does not develop his account of aesthetic autonomy there in order to separate private aesthetic experience from the public political sphere, but rather to unite them. For Schiller, the aesthetic sphere is supposed to jointly and simultaneously develop individual subjectivity and the collective political state. Schiller is misunderstood on this point because his theoretical project seems to immediately run into the following basic paradox. If the aesthetic state is one of indeterminacy, then being *in* the aesthetic state of mind would mean being *outside* of the political state of affairs of the everyday world of determinate causes and effects. How then could there be any connection between the aesthetic and political spheres?

This same paradox emerges in the various forms of contemporary social theory that turn to textual indeterminacy as a solution to totalizing political ideology. For example, in *Hegemony and Socialist Strategy: Towards a Radical Democratic Politics*, Ernesto Laclau and Chantal Mouffe present textual indeterminacy as a model of freedom from all previous ideological categories and determinations, and thus as the basis for radical democracy.[3] But the Schillerian problem of aesthetic autonomy returns with a vengeance: how can one connect indeterminacy (whether aesthetic or textual) with actual political practices? Moving from an indeterminate state to the determinate political state would require reifying categories and imposing limits and determinations. The movement out of the aesthetic sphere would therefore entail losing whatever freedom that seemed to be found there. It is from this perspective that the appeal to textual indeterminacy runs the risk of shifting from *being the basis of* actual radical democracy to *being in lieu of* actual radical democracy.

In order to engage this continuing problematic relationship between the aesthetic and political spheres, this book will examine the Romantic origins and later trajectory of what I call *aesthetic statism*. I will argue that Schiller thought he could escape the paradox seemingly inherent in the project of connecting the aesthetic and political spheres because he based his account of the aesthetic sphere on the unique, mediating structure of the Romantic symbol. This structure is best expressed by

Coleridge's description of the symbol in *The Statesman's Manual*, in which he describes it as that which "abides itself as a living part" in a "Unity," while "it enunciates the whole"(*SM*, 30). Through this mediating logic of the symbol, both Schiller and Coleridge purport to reconcile the opposition between individual subjectivity and the objective political state.

The same reconciling role for the aesthetic sphere can be seen in Matthew Arnold's and John Ruskin's Victorian pronouncements on culture and society. And like the aesthetic sphere and the symbol, Arnold's and Ruskin's conceptions of culture can be traced to roots in the Romantic era. As I will discuss in my first chapter, during the Romantic period in England and Germany, opposing conceptions of the nation and the state developed alongside two correspondingly opposing conceptions of culture. On the one hand, culture was identified with what came to be called high culture and was seen as a universal canon of the best that has been thought and said. On the other hand, culture also became identified with an anthropological model of particular national cultures. In a series of complicated ways, the liberal state became tied to the concept of universal high culture, while the cultural nation became tied to the concept of national culture. Aesthetic statism as I will analyze it in this book is the variously formulated attempts of Friedrich Schiller, Samuel Taylor Coleridge, Matthew Arnold, and John Ruskin to reconcile the opposing models of culture and the nation/state through the mediation of the aesthetic sphere. According to aesthetic statism, the harmonious relationship both between individual subjects and the political state, and between particular national cultures and universal reason is predicated on the reconciliation of the particular and the universal embodied in the Romantic symbol.

Outside of the school of cultural criticism inaugurated by Raymond Williams, however, the tradition of aesthetic statism has largely been ignored in contemporary literary theory.[4] In the case of Coleridge's seminal account of the symbol, criticism has tended to follow Paul de Man in viewing it in terms of the rhetorical figure of synecdoche (the identification of part and whole), while ignoring the political issues involved in a synecdochal account of the state.[5] The Romantic lineage of Arnold's project in the symbolic state theory of Coleridge and Schiller is even less known in literary critical circles. Even though Matthew Arnold is routinely acknowledged to be the guiding presence of modern English literary criticism, the significance of his identification of culture and the state in *Culture and Anarchy* (1869) generally goes unmentioned even in the midst of the current emphasis on the politics of literature.[6] The critical climate is therefore right to analyze the central connections between Romanticism, aesthetics, and political theory embodied in the tradition of aesthetic statism.[7]

SCOPE AND TRAJECTORY

In recognizing and attempting to overcome the split in the human condition between subjective and objective, and particular and universal, the theorists of aesthetic statism were participating within what is now described as the discourse of the crisis of modernity. Thus, as I will detail in my first chapter, the lineage of aesthetic statism and, indeed, the political context of Romanticism itself is only explicable within the set of issues bound up with the concept of modernity. Since the development and crises of modernity form the conceptual backdrop to this book, I do not limit myself to authors and texts between 1798 and 1832, nor to a traditional Romantic canon of works. Although the category of *modernity* seems broad, its benefit is that it can delineate continuities between writers which are masked by traditional labels such as Enlightenment, Romantic, Idealist, or Victorian. However, it is important to add that because I approach modernity from the specific perspective of aesthetic statism, this book is not designed to nor does it purport to present a comprehensive account of all the issues and texts involved in the concept of modernity.

Likewise, although I discuss the theoretical underpinnings of the liberal state and the cultural nation, this book is not meant to be an exhaustive treatment of the nations or states as historical and theoretical entities, nor is the book intended as an exhaustive comparative study of England and Germany on these questions. My intention in moving between England and Germany is to reveal connections between these theorists of aesthetic statism, connections that would not be evident if these writers were read only from within their individual national traditions. The book takes Schiller's account of the aesthetic state and Coleridge's account of the symbol as its central theoretical paradigms. I discuss my central figures by examining how these paradigms are expressed in formulations that reflect the particularities of each theorist's individual and national situation. And although I have tried to be scrupulous in defining and respecting historical influences and the integrity of literary genres and national traditions, I must admit that the guiding sensibility of this work is that of the literary theorist and political philosopher who criss-crosses all such ultimately arbitrary boundaries in search of a comprehensive perspective.

By coining the term *aesthetic statism*, however, I do not propose to designate a shared monolithic philosophy. The differences between each theorist can be as significant as their similarities. But overall it is possible to define four central elements that aesthetic statism seeks to connect: (1) the aesthetic sphere, with its essential autonomy and underlying logic of the symbol; (2) individual autonomous subjectivity and its formation (*Bildung*); (3) the enlightenment conception of universal reason; and (4) the political state and its formation. I give an overview of these elements in my first two chapters. If these central elements cease to harmonize, aesthetic statism breaks apart, and indeed the trajectory that this book traces from Schiller to contemporary theory is that of a disintegration of Schiller's ambitious unifying theory.

Everything after Schiller represents a theoretical weakening of his original aspirations for aesthetic statism to hold these four elements in harmony. Coleridge comes the closest to maintaining the theoretical ambitions of the Schillerian project, but his commitment to preserving the traditional English constitution comes into conflict with the highest aspirations of autonomous subjectivity as expressed by Schiller. Arnold's explicit refusal to mount a metaphysical defense of the aesthetic leads to a contradictory account of culture, one that, as I will argue, silently continues to inform contemporary literary criticism. The early Ruskin bases the moral guidance of art on the symbolism of beauty, but moves towards a sociological account that undercuts the ability of art to serve as a guide to society. In an attempt to regain that guiding role for the aesthetic, the later Ruskin presents a gendered aesthetic sphere that ends up reinforcing traditional social and sexual hierarchies. It is within this context of the increasing rift between the different elements of aesthetic statism that I analyze the twentieth-century theorists Theodor Adorno and Jürgen Habermas. Both Adorno and Habermas are heirs to Schiller's project in the *Aesthetic Letters*. But while Schiller sought to integrate the aesthetic with reason, Adorno and Habermas face the dichotomy of the aesthetic *or* reason. Their attempts to navigate that dichotomy form the focus of the seventh chapter.

In order to give a better preliminary sense of the specific focus of this book, let me briefly relate it to two works that deal with many of the same issues: Raymond Williams' *Culture and Society*, which focuses on the English literary and philosophical tradition, and Josef Chytry's *The Aesthetic State*, which focuses on the German one.[8] Williams' book lays the groundwork for any discussion of the intersection of culture and society, and his work is both a model and an inspiration for me, as it has been for many others. Obviously, I have not set out to produce a more comprehensive account: I only discuss a handful of the English writers that Williams does, namely, Coleridge, Mill, Arnold, and Ruskin. What I am trying to add to his discussion of culture and society is a sustained, theoretically articulated, account of the way the symbol and the aesthetic sphere have been utilized as reconciling mediums for the contradictions of political modernity. For, although he masterfully defines Coleridge's position in the English tradition of culture and society, Williams does not discuss Coleridge's account of the symbol. Now that Coleridge's prose writings are widely available through the publication of *The Collected Works of Samuel Taylor Coleridge*, a more extensive analysis of Coleridge's later prose is required to do justice to his contribution to the discourse of culture and society. Furthermore, while in later works Williams goes on to engage continental theory, *Culture and Society* focuses exclusively on the English tradition. I have sought therefore to revisit the English writers in the context of a theoretical perspective informed by the Coleridgean symbol and the Schillerian aesthetic sphere in a way that is relevant to contemporary discussions of both literary and social theory.

Chytry's intellectual history, *The Aesthetic State*, focuses on the German tradition of attempting to revive the ideals of the aesthetic state of the ancient Greeks. The originating figure in this tradition is Winckelmann, and Chytry traces his influence on the Weimar aesthetic humanism that culminates in Schiller's account in the *Aesthetic Letters*. From there, he discusses the impact of this tradition on the idealist philosophies of Hölderlin, Hegel, and Schelling, and on what he calls the "realist" philosophies of Marx, Wagner, Nietzsche, Heidegger, and Marcuse. Once again, my handling of the German tradition is more selective than comprehensive, and, again, that principle of selection has been according to the reconciling model of the symbol. For, although Chytry notes the idea of the synthesis of concrete and universal in the work of art, he never discusses the symbol or the literary and philosophical discussions surrounding it. He focuses rather on the fusion of concrete and universal in social enactments such as religious rituals, drama, and dance.

Chytry's analysis of the Greek ideal and the role of drama provides a valuable complementary context, especially for Schiller, and I generally agree with his conclusions about the German tradition. However, I tend to use the term "aesthetic statism" more narrowly than he uses the term "aesthetic state," and the reasons underlying this are reflected in the different way each of us views Hegel's place in this tradition. For Chytry, Hegel is the preeminent philosopher of the aesthetic state. And while I certainly consider Hegel a central aesthetic philosopher, I do not consider him an aesthetic statist in the same way that Schiller, Coleridge, Arnold, Ruskin, and Adorno are. For, whereas all of these thinkers explicitly foreground aesthetic models throughout their mature work, Hegel's mature work subordinates aesthetics to philosophy.

Chytry does acknowledge that Hegel abandons the aesthetic state ideal of ancient Greece for the modern rational state model of the *Philosophy of Right*. But Chytry argues that Hegel's commitment to the aesthetic state continues on in the aesthetic form of his dialectical philosophy.[9] Since Hegel's dialectic philosophy concerns the reconciliation of subjective and objective, I agree that the structure of Hegel's dialectic can be seen as analogous to the kind of aesthetic reconciliation embodied in the symbol and the aesthetic sphere. Hegel himself is well aware of this analogy and expresses it in his earlier Schiller-inspired work. But it seems quite significant to me that, given this awareness, he nonetheless goes out of his way to distinguish philosophy from art in his mature work, and to make philosophy, not art, the guide to the state. I am open to the argument that Hegel and indeed all political philosophers in the dialectical tradition might *implicitly* be using aesthetic models of reconciliation and thus might be viewed as implicit aesthetic statists. But I want to focus this book on thinkers who *explicitly* profess the guiding importance of the aesthetic sphere to the political sphere. Defining aesthetic statism in this way considerably narrows the list.

MOTIVATIONS

At the outset, my selection of Schiller, Coleridge, Arnold, Ruskin, and Adorno will appear plausible enough to the reader, since these writers are all known to be aesthetic theorists with strong interests in social theory. However, this book also includes discussions of topics that might not seem at first glance to concern aesthetic issues, such as the opposition between the cultural nation and liberal state (in chapter 1), the Victorian domestic sphere (in chapter 6), and Habermas' theory of the public sphere and communicative action (in chapter 7). My rationale for discussing these topics is part of the dual orientation of this book as a work in both Romantic literary theory and social theory. As an initial way of explaining my choice and treatment of these materials here, I would like to sketch out my motivations both as a Romanticist and as a social theorist and indicate how the two combined in the writing of this book.

I have long been interested in European theory and continental constructions of Romanticism, but when I began this project I was frustrated with the extreme apolitical aestheticism of de Manian deconstruction, which was then the prevalent manifestation of continental theory in academic Romantic studies. Consequently, I enthusiastically greeted the move towards new historical and "political" approaches to Romanticism in the 1980s. But I noticed that the new wave of critics making the appeal to history and politics often ended up perpetuating the same apolitical view of canonical Romanticism. Many of these critics either evoked the categories of history and politics to criticize canonical Romanticism for its attempt to retreat into an aesthetic world, or they used them in order to make the case for including new works in the canon, particularly works by women writers of the Romantic period. There was little recognition that a concern with the political was an integral part of the discourse on the aesthetic by canonical Romantic writers such as Schiller and Coleridge. The further irony was that, despite all the talk of expanding the Romantic canon, theoretical arguments about the politics of Romanticism still seemed to be largely based on readings of the most traditional genre in that canon, lyric poetry. The great body of explicit aesthetic theory which bears on the political in prose works of the Romantic tradition went largely unmentioned. (My reactions to these developments in Romantic studies informs the discussion of Romantic criticism in the first chapter of this book.)

Just as I was dissatisfied with the prevailing treatment of political theory in Romanticism studies, so too I was dissatisfied with the prevailing treatment of the issue of subjectivity in theoretical circles. Too often, these discussions were simply ritualized demonstrations of the "death of the modern subject" with little or no awareness of how the critique of subjectivity was originally connected to Marx's analysis of subjectivity as the basis of bourgeois political ideology. What had once been a critique with recognizable political implications had now become another metaphor for aesthetic indeterminacy. In my view, if one is to engage meaningfully in a critique of subjectivity one needs to address the philosophical and political contexts within which the powerful critiques of bourgeois subjectivity were originally mounted by Marx and continued by later thinkers such as the theorists of the Frankfurt school.

But while I acknowledge the value of interrogating the pretensions of bourgeois subjectivity, I am also committed to retaining the concept of individual agency, which is the essential element of the liberal democratic political tradition. In social theory, I have gravitated towards the work of Habermas, since he appears to be the only major contemporary theorist who seeks to make a case for reforming rather than rejecting the central elements of the liberal tradition of subjectivity – individuality, rationality, and a noncoercive public sphere. These were likewise the elements that Schiller, Coleridge, and Arnold sought to ground through their aesthetic statism. In the tradition that this book traces, models of the aesthetic and culture are connected to the process of the development of individual self-consciousness. However, what the tradition of aesthetic statism seeks to develop is individual, but not individual*istic*, rationality. In opposition to the atomized individualistic subjectivity of classical English liberalism, aesthetic statism seeks a model of individual consciousness that is instrinsically integrated within a larger social and political structure, a structure which they identify with the state. This I would argue represents the central connection of Habermas' work to the tradition of aesthetic statism. Habermas continues this tradition through his arguments that the public sphere and the process of communicative action underlying that public sphere are the structures through which the political state can transform its laws from *de facto* political domination to the rational consent of the individuals that form the state. I have therefore concluded this study by attempting to assess how much of the tradition of aesthetic statism can be retained within Habermas' accounts of the public sphere and communicative action.

I am aware that the whole tradition of aesthetic statism I describe from Schiller through Habermas, which attempts to describe a unifying basis of the political state, will be viewed with suspicion by those contemporary supporters of the diverse and the local who regard any appeal to the universal as intrinsically oppressive to particular constituencies. And while the analysis of the thinkers in this study constantly returns to the issue of the conflict between the universal and the particular, this book does not have the space nor is its primary purpose to provide a general sustained defense in contemporary terms of the value of the concept of a common public sphere. For this, readers can turn to Habermas himself and the vast literature that supports or condemns his project.

Without therefore being able to fill out the arguments, I will simply state where I stand in terms of the contemporary debates on this issue. My position is that it is time to challenge the all-too-easy way that diversity has been celebrated as intrinsically emancipating and the all-too-easy way that any appeal to a common ground of understanding has been attacked as totalitarian. In much contemporary theory, terms like *the local* and *diversity* have become abstract goods-in-themselves. But I would argue that one does not get very far if the discussion remains on the level of debating the general value of diversity as an abstract social good. One has to specify the kinds of diversity one wants and their relation to a vision of the good of the social whole. Conversely, the relevant issue should not be simply whether a common ground of meaning is being appealed to, but rather the basis and the reason for that appeal.

The rejection of the universal and the celebration of the local are presented in many contemporary theoretical circles as the only path to political emancipation. But I would argue that universal processes are at work whether one theoretically approves of the universal or not, and they cannot be checked by merely appealing to particularity. Today, we can see two apparently opposing processes going on simultaneously, an increasingly totalizing administered global uniformity of economic and political systems (developments associated with *modernity*), accompanied with an ever-increasing proliferation of cultural identifications and cultural commodities (developments associated with *postmodernity*). Rather than challenging the totalizing processes of globalization, however, this proliferation of cultural identities and commodities has been integrated within the system. In this globalized world, we get more, but more of the same everywhere in the world.

Given this scenario, I would argue that theoretical positions that celebrate the local and the diverse, but also deny or give up on the possibility of finding any ground of unity in that diversity, may in fact have the consequence (intended or not) of allowing the continued progress of these damaging totalizing processes now associated with globalization. Because such theoretical positions exclude any positive role for the universal, they also exclude the possibility of a structure such as the public sphere that could resist or regulate the negative universality reflected in global totalizing processes. A theoretical position that explicitly strives to find a *noncoercive* basis of unity in diversity, such as Habermas has sought to, may in fact be what is necessary to provide the conceptual and political grounds to resist these totalizing processes. In writing this book I have sought therefore not only to trace historically a particular line of thinking about the relationship between aesthetics and political subjectivity, but to advocate what remains valuable and viable in this line of thought at the present time.

CHAPTER I

Modernity, subjectivity, liberalism, and nationalism

THE POLITICS OF ROMANTICISM

In English language criticism, the place to begin the discussion of the political context of Romanticism is with the work of Raymond Williams. His account of Coleridge in *Culture and Society* lays out the essential terms of discussion:

> Coleridge's emphasis in his social writings is on *institutions*. The promptings to perfection came indeed from "the cultivated heart" – that is to say, from man's inward consciousness – but, as Burke before him, Coleridge insisted on man's need for institutions which should confirm and constitute his personal efforts. Cultivation, in fact, though an inward was never a merely individual process.¹

Williams' account of Coleridge presents us both with opposing terms, "institutions" versus "man's inward consciousness," and with the means of overcoming that opposition through "cultivation," that is, through the medium of culture. As a Marxist, Williams was critical of the conservative elements of Coleridge's political writings, but as a sociologist of knowledge, Williams agreed with Coleridge's key point that institutions and subjectivity are vitally interrelated. Indeed Williams argues in *Culture and Society* that an opposition between institutions and subjectivity developed throughout the nineteenth century, and that this opposition radically transformed the concept of culture. For Williams, the worldview of the Romantic period, exemplified by Coleridge, is characterized precisely by its lack of such an opposition:

> The supposed opposition between attention to natural beauty and attention to government, or between personal feeling and the nature of man in society, is on the whole a later development. What were seen at the end of the nineteenth century as disparate interests, between which a man must choose and in the act of choice declare himself poet or sociologist, were, normally, at the beginning of the century, seen as interlocking interests: a conclusion about personal feeling

became a conclusion about society, and an observation of natural beauty carried a necessary moral reference to the whole unified life of man. *Culture and Society*, 30

However, the tendency in modern criticism of Romanticism has been to place the separation between subjectivity and society squarely in the Romantic period itself rather than locate it, as Williams does, later in the century. The history of modern criticism of Romanticism is precisely one of the dichotomizing and privileging of one of these terms over the other: institutions *or* consciousness, politics *or* subjectivity. One can see this in M. H. Abrams' summation in *Natural Supernaturalism* (1971), which emphasizes subjectivity at the expense of institutions: "The Romantic poets were not *complete* poets, in that they represent little of the social dimension of human experience; for although they insist on the importance of community, they express this matter largely as a profound need of the individual consciousness."[2]

The difference between Williams and Abrams can be attributed in large part to a different conception of what texts constitute Romanticism. Although Abrams presents a model of Romanticism based on German philosophical texts, he never analyzes the equally philosophical but politically oriented later prose of Coleridge such as *The Friend* or *Constitution of Church and State*. These are precisely the texts Williams foregrounds in his interpretation of Romanticism. As in any field of study, there is a reciprocal relationship between its theoretical concepts and its canon of texts. Thus, it is because Abrams regards Romantic subjectivity as essentially opposed to social issues that he can deem certain poems (primarily the short lyrics and *The Prelude*) and certain philosophical texts (Hegel's *Phenomenology*) representative of Romanticism, while seeing others as essentially non-Romantic (Wordsworth's *Excursion* or Coleridge's later prose), even though they issue from the same writers and the same philosophical traditions.[3]

Such a view of isolated Romantic subjectivity is not limited to the "traditional" Romantic paradigm of Abrams. It is also evident in the major Deconstructionist critics of Romanticism, Geoffrey Hartman and Paul de Man. Like Abrams, Hartman places Wordsworthian subjectivity in the context of European, and especially German, philosophic thought.[4] In *Wordsworth's Poetry, 1787–1814* (following the paradigm of his earlier *Unmediated Vision*), Hartman stresses the isolation of Wordsworth's subjectivity as it pulls back from nature at crucial moments. And while Paul de Man is now generally identified with an emphasis on the text as the final level of analysis, isolated subjectivity is the central issue of his influential essay "The Rhetoric of Temporality."[5]

What might be called a new historical movement in Romantic studies has criticized both Abrams and Deconstruction precisely for foregrounding subjectivity in Romanticism at the expense of social and political analysis. For example, in her essay "Plotting the Revolution: The Political Narrative of Romantic Poetry and Criticism," Marilyn Butler has argued against Abrams' assumption that German philosophic models of subjectivity are the keys to understanding English Romanticism. In challenging this, she has also challenged the critical corollaries that Wordsworth, because he is the poet of such subjectivity, should be considered the central figure of English Romanticism, and that *The Prelude*, as his manifesto of subjectivity, should be considered its central text:

> The high road of English poetry during the French Revolutionary wars was, we know, of quite another kind: it had to do not with retirement in pursuit of what – the self? God? – but with nationhood and power . . . What we now call English Romanticism . . . had to do with the characterization of the central state – that way of coming to terms with the "platoon" to which we belong, in Burke's word, when the degree to which we *do* belong is in real doubt.[6]

Butler seems to agree with Raymond Williams in focusing on Burke and arguing that Romanticism must be understood in terms of institutions (the "platoon"). But, unlike Williams and like Abrams, she reinstates the same opposition between subjectivity and institutions. Butler and Abrams both begin with the same basic opposition between subjectivity and politics, a dichotomy that defines subjectivity in terms of a retreat from the world. However, while Butler agrees with Abrams in identifying this isolated subjectivity with German philosophy, she draws different conclusions about the relationship between German philosophy and English Romanticism. For Abrams, English Romanticism is romantic because it shares the worldview of German idealism; for Butler, English Romanticism is English precisely because it does not.

Certainly, English Romanticism must be read in light of English history and contexts (as I will do so in this study), but in her reaction against the hegemony of German philosophical models Butler ends up recreating an attitude all too familiar to Coleridgeans, the traditional "common-sense" English attitude that rejects German metaphysics out of hand as otherworldly, abstract, and un-English.[7] In order to oppose this general assumption that the issue of subjectivity is inherently incompatible with social and political issues, I want to return to and amplify Raymond Williams' assertion that "cultivation . . . though an inward was never a merely individual process." Furthermore, I will argue that this assertion is true not only for English Romanticism but for the German philosophical tradition of subjectivity that has been regarded as setting up the opposition between subjectivity and the political world in the first place. The context in which I will locate the interrelations between subjectivity and political formation is in the very concept of modernity, which presents itself both as a historical and a philosophical problem.

SUBJECTIVITY AND THE CRISES OF MODERNITY

The term *modernity* has perhaps as many meanings as the term *Romanticism* and it is not my intention to describe all of them here. In discussing modernity, one has to be careful to distinguish several elements that are often linked together: (1) modern subjectivity, (2) mass political emancipation and democratization, and (3) the material processes of modernization involved in the development of the modern bourgeois state, including bureaucratization and modes of modern capitalist production, particularly the division of labor. In certain English *laissez-faire* liberal accounts like that of John Stuart Mill, these three elements are ultimately seen as going hand in hand. But, as we will see, the theorists of aesthetic statism often judge each element distinctly. The understanding of modernity that I will be initially describing here stresses the first element, modern subjectivity, as the heart of the development and crises of modernity, and considers the second and third elements primarily in relation to it. This is the understanding of the classical German philosophical tradition of Kant, Schiller, and Hegel. With Marx, Max Weber, and the Frankfurt school, the balance changes, and subjectivity and the possibility of political emancipation are viewed rather as depending on the third element, that is, the material processes of modernization.

The concept of modern subjectivity provides the context that connects Enlightenment and Romanticism, the two great cultural movements that are usually set in opposition to each other. And while this element of modernity is particularly identified with the German philosophical tradition, it is also present in crucial English theorists such as Coleridge and Arnold, both of whom were informed by a variety of continental sources. In my summary here, I will particularly be drawing on the account formulated by Habermas in his history and critique of modernity in *Philosophical Discourse of Modernity*. According to Habermas, the emergence of autonomous subjectivity is the defining feature of the philosophical and historical concept of modernity. Along with and connected to the development of autonomous subjectivity, modernity is further defined by the development of universalistic reason, the constitutional state, and autonomous art. According to Kant's original aspirations for enlightenment, the modern subject has its origin in its emancipation from the oppressive forces that had previously held it in bondage: ignorance, superstition, and the causal nexus of nature. Subjectivity strives to liberate itself from the systems of false thought and the causal determinations of natural forces that confine it. But in doing so, subjectivity also initiates a crisis. In liberating itself from oppressive totalizing forces, subjectivity also runs the risk of splitting itself off from those totalities that give its life meaning.

This is the context in which Habermas describes Hegel's attempt to solve traditional philosophical oppositions through his dialectical philosophy. These philosophical oppositions represent the contradictions that an isolated subjectivity faces in the condition of modernity: "by criticizing the philosophical oppositions – nature and spirit, sensibility and understanding, understanding and reason, theoretical and practical reason, judgment and imagination, I and non-I, finite and infinite, knowledge and faith – [Hegel] wants to respond to the crisis of the diremption of life itself" (*PD*, 21). This is why for Hegel, and the philosophical discourse of modernity that Hegel helps to define, "the critique of subjective idealism is at the same time a critique of modernity" (*PD*, 21).

As a solution to these crises of modernity, the early Hegel looked to a "mythopoetic version of a reconciliation of modernity" (*PD*, 22), a project he shared with Hölderlin and Schelling.[8] These attempts, however, remained tied to models of the past – such as the polis of ancient Greece and the Incarnation of primitive Christianity. But since Hegel felt the situation of modernity to be in some fundamental sense new and unprecedented, in a word, modern, he ultimately had to reject using the solutions of the past to solve the crises of the present. In the *Phenomenology of Spirit*, Hegel turns to subjectivity itself, what he calls absolute spirit, to overcome the crises engendered by modern subjectivity. This is a turn, Habermas argues, that has defined the central paradox within any philosophical project based on a philosophy of consciousness paradigm to solve the crises of modernity.

Since modern subjectivity defines itself in reaction to the structures of the past, the next question becomes what social and political structures are suitable for the modern moment, and by what basis shall they be judged? For Hegel the criterion is reason, and he posited an identity between modernity and rationality. The modern moment was defined as the progress of the subject towards absolute knowledge and, correspondingly, political freedom. In Hegel's *Philosophy of Right*, the modern state (epitomized by Hegel's Prussia) is presented as the culmination of reason, a place where the subject finds freedom within an ethical totality (*Sittlichkeit*) that gives that freedom meaning. Hegel's account of the Prussian state as the culmination of reason was famously criticized by Marx in his *Critique of Hegel's Philosophy of Right*, in the course of which Marx proposed turning Hegel's dialectic on its head. But although Marx thus changed the terms of the dialectic of history from a spiritual to a material basis, he continued Hegel's identification of modernity with rationality. Marx's materialist dialectic continued the model of the movement of history as the process of the realization of increasingly more rational structures, culminating in the inevitable development of world communism.

A challenge to the identification of modernity and rationality was mounted by Max Weber's work on the processes of modernization. Weber's studies detailed the distinct features of modernization in the West, but while these processes were defined by a distinct logic, Weber cast doubt on whether they were rational in the traditional ethical sense of tending towards the greater human good, the sense that Hegel and Marx had assumed in their identifications of rationality and modernization. Weber's analysis of capitalism and its origins in the Protestant work ethic showed a system of accumulation whose logic of endless accumulation and expansion had completely separated itself from its original ideological justifications and become an end in itself. The paradox that Weber's work brought into sharp focus was the fact that although modernity begins with the goal of emancipating the individual subject, the material processes of modernization, as they are institutionalized in modern economic, political, and scientific structures, work towards destroying those very ways of life that are required to sustain individual subjectivity. This is the paradox vividly illustrated by Horkheimer and Adorno's *Dialectic of Enlightenment*, and explored in some form by all the thinkers associated with the Frankfurt school tradition of critical theory, particularly Habermas, whose own theories of the public sphere and communicative action are specifically formulated as attempts to address this problem.

As I have summarized it here, this Habermasian paradigm of the crisis of modernity is applicable in many ways to English writers such as Coleridge, Arnold, and Ruskin. But there are some differences. As we saw, in the German tradition Hegel identifies the modern moment with the dual perfection of reason and the state. But Coleridge crucially defines English reactions to modernity through his influential distinction between "civilization" and "cultivation" in *Church and State*. Coleridge's intention is precisely to distinguish the elements that Hegel had sought to identify: the material processes of modernity and spiritual perfection. "Civilization," in the sense of the economic development of the bourgeois state, does not for Coleridge go hand in hand with "cultivation," the spiritual progression of society, because, for him, the spiritual state of a nation does not necessarily advance with its economic and bureaucratic development. Thus, the most prominent and influential English reactions to modernity as expressed by Coleridge, Arnold, and especially Ruskin contain at the outset a significant strand of antimodern sentiment.

However, this is not to say that there is no such antimodern strand in German thought. As we will see, in the *Aesthetic Letters* Schiller starts by precisely asserting that the spiritual crisis of contemporary society results from the fragmenting trends of modernity, in particular the division of labor. But as a generalization (although open to many qualifications) one can say that the Germans from Schiller to Hegel celebrate modernity as the fulfillment of their utopian aspirations, even though, and perhaps especially because, they have not yet experienced the full material effects of modernization. The English thinkers of the period from Coleridge through Ruskin, who are in the midst of experiencing the most advanced case of modernization yet seen in the world, are more cautious and critical of modernity and tend to celebrate the premodern structures that modernization is in the act of destroying.

Another difference between the English and German traditions is in their attitude towards reason as the emancipatory element of modernity. For Schiller and the mainstream of the German philosophical tradition in general, the key to the utopian possibilities of modernity is the proper application of reason. In Schiller's case, it is the application of reason in conjunction with the aesthetic sphere. As for the negative aspects of modernity, the basic attitude of the German tradition is summed up in Habermas' slogan that the answer to the problems of the Enlightenment is not less, but more enlightenment. But, as we will see, while Coleridge is committed to reason and the values of the Enlightenment, he expresses this commitment through a conservative English nationalist perspective that looks to premodern traditions as the proper embodiments of reason. Similarly, while Arnold calls for the "sweetness and light" he associates with the free play of reason, he tends to find that the best expressions of reason are already embodied in traditional forms and establishments. And while Ruskin is the most radical in his criticism of contemporary political economy, he looks to the hierarchies of the past, not the mass democracies of the future, for his vision of the proper state.

THE LIBERAL STATE AND THE CULTURAL NATION

The period from the late eighteenth century through the middle of the nineteenth is the time of the development of modern conceptions and structures of the liberal state and the cultural nation. As Carl Woodring reminds us, both of these political movements have been connected to Romanticism: "Just as most literary historians continue to associate romanticism with liberalism and revolt, by a linkage already popular when Babbitt and Hulme made it a focus of attack, so with a flip of the coin social scientists, with large obligations to European and especially German thought, currently associate romanticism with conservatism, reaction, or the totalitarian State."[9] The reason that Romanticism has been identified with two seemingly opposed political movements lies in the fact that both of these movements are responses to the crisis of modern subjectivity that we have discussed above. And indeed one can locate a concept that runs through both political movements and which is identified with Romanticism through its participation in the discourse of modernity. This is the central concept of modern subjectivity, *autonomous self-determination*, which carries with it the corollary notion of achieving freedom through casting off the restraints of oppressive external forces.[10] In Romantic discourse, both literary and political, this principle is expressed in narratives of beings striving after and developing their own particular genius by following the call of their own inward rules. The difference between liberalism and cultural nationalism is that for liberalism the being striving to obtain autonomy is an individual, while for cultural nationalism it is a whole people.

Especially in modern English language usage, much of the distinguishing force has been lost between the words *state* and *nation*. Indeed for most of the twentieth century these two words have been seen as converging, as evidenced by the standard political hybrid term, the *nation-state*. But they have distinct political logics that were felt and understood by those contemporary theorists who sought to reconcile their oppositions. For example, from his vantage point mid-century, John Stuart Mill begins *Considerations on Representative Government* (1861) by summarizing what he sees as the "two conflicting theories respecting political institutions" that have dominated political speculation up to his time.[11] The first type of theory regards forms of government as "wholly an affair of invention and contrivance": "Being made by man, it is assumed that man has the choice either to make them or not, and how or on what pattern they shall be made" (*RG*, 374). The opposing school holds that "the fundamental political institutions of a people are . . . a sort of organic growth from the nature and life of that people: a product of their habits, instincts, and unconscious wants and desires, scarcely at all of their deliberate purposes" (*RG*, 374–5). The first position clearly summarizes the tradition of the liberal state and English social contract theory, specifically the reformist Utilitarianism of Mill's father, James Mill, and Jeremy Bentham. The second position describes the cultural nationalism and continental historicism that Mill had previously identified with the "the Germano-Coleridgian doctrine" in his 1840 essay on Coleridge.[12] For Mill, the next step in political theory required reconciling these seemingly opposed political philosophies. This is precisely the project that Schiller, Coleridge, Arnold, and Ruskin had undertaken in their projects of aesthetic statism, and we will turn to the specifics of their attempts in the chapters that follow. But it is important at the outset to understand the contrasting logics of these opposing solutions to the problem of the modern subject.

Liberalism views government as an invention of individuals created through rational agreements (social contracts, whether actual or implied), and thus treats the state as an entity that can and should be amended through appeals to universal reason and universal human rights. Cultural nationalism, on the other hand, views the nation as an organic outgrowth of a people, a *Volk*. The cultural nation is the political embodiment of the national culture of the people. This national culture is seen as constituting the people, rather than being constituted *by* a people, as it is in liberal theory.[13] The unity of the cultural nation is based on the concept of *common culture*, that is, shared historical and social cultural practices centered around a common language, literature, ethnic practices, religion, and even race insofar as it is tied to the former.[14] The cultural nation is grounded on the ideas of cultural difference and self-determination. According to this, the cultural nation strives to express its unique identity, to form itself autonomously and follow the lead of its inward being.[15] Since each subject of this nation is the embodiment of a cultural type, of which the cultural nation itself is the most complete expression, there should be no separation between individual and group subjectivity, between public and private spheres.[16] Thus extreme forms of cultural nationalism finally recognize only *one form of subjectivity*, that of the cultural nation itself.[17] For a cultural nationalist, a separate individual subjectivity is identified with the liberal individuality that is seen as the main affliction of modernity. Liberal subjectivity is treated precisely as an illusion to be dispelled or as a problem to be solved through the appeal to common culture and to the cultural origins of the nation. Conversely, it is precisely the separation between individual and group subjectivity that theories of the liberal state seek to maintain. The problem of liberal state theory is the problem of maintaining individual identities within the collectivity of the state. Liberal state theory takes individual subjectivity as a necessary and positive result of modernity, not, as cultural nationalism often views it, as a symptom of the disintegration of authentic social unity caused by the fragmenting processes of modernity.

LIBERALISM AND NATIONALISM IN ENGLAND AND GERMANY

As we see in Mill's description, in the cases of England and Germany, the tendency has been to identify England with liberalism, and Germany with nationalism. The traditional historical explanation for this is the differences in political development between the two countries. In short, at the beginning of the nineteenth century, England was a unified political state, while Germany was striving to become one. The decay of the Holy Roman Empire led to the political localism that characterized Germany in the eighteenth century. In 1766, the Empire was split up into 314 territories and towns and into 1,475 free lordships.[18] In contrast, formal political unity had already been achieved in England by the Acts of Union beginning and ending the eighteenth century, and England's political unity and stability were already supposed to be cemented by the set of documents known collectively as "the Constitution."[19]

Theories of nationalism, like those of Kedourie, have maintained that nationalism is fueled by the goal of making the political state identical with the cultural nation. Germany is usually seen as the paradigmatic example because, while the Germans had a unified sense of themselves as a cultural nation of German-speaking peoples, this cultural nation was divided up in multiple political states. In contrast, by virtue of its early political unification, Britain is usually seen as not having gone through a nationalistic phase. Recent historical scholarship has however disputed this traditional view. Gerald Newman has challenged the accepted account that England had no nationalistic phase, and Linda Colley has shown just how much work it took to forge a popular sense of shared British national identity out of the distinct ethnicities of England, Scotland, and Wales after the Acts of Union had supposedly politically unified the country.[20] Newman's cultural history of nationalism in England is particularly relevant to the context in which the political orientation of English Romanticism should be viewed. He suggests the origin of English nationalism in the period from 1740 to 1789 was a reaction against the French-dominated cosmopolitan culture of the English aristocracy. According to Newman, the ideology of English nationalism becomes the vehicle through which those excluded from aristocratic circles could claim their share of political power. Thus for Newman the rejection of France by Wordsworth and Coleridge after the French Revolution and their subsequent embrace of English nationalism signals not a retreat into conservatism, but rather an embrace of the true socially progressive force of the age.[21]

Conversely, while historiography has usually neglected the presence of nationalism in England, intellectual history has usually neglected the presence of liberalism in the German philosophical tradition. Because of the horrors of German fascism in this century, the tendency has been to cast the shadow back into history and view any German pronouncements on nationalism and the state as forerunners of Nazi totalitarianism. In particular, German Romanticism, with its models of organic national unity, has been seen as irredeemably opposed to liberalism. But this view has been challenged by Frederick Beiser in his recent revisionist account of the politics of German Romanticism, in which he analyzes Novalis and Friedrich Schlegel and argues that within the contemporary political context of their time, these figures were radical rather than, as is often believed, conservative.[22] In an argument similar to Newman's about the progressive force of English nationalism, Beiser states that the appeal to the organic nation by German Romanticism was a revolutionary attack against the unethical order of the *ancien régime*. It is from this political perspective that Beiser asserts, "Romanticism was the aesthetics of republicanism" (*Enlightenment, Revolution, and Romanticism*, 260).

While Newman's and Beiser's arguments about the progressive implications of nationalism viewed with their contemporary political context are persuasive, from the perspective of traditional Anglo-American liberalism, one is still left with the problem of reconciling the political determination of a people with the inalienable political rights of the individual. As I have indicated in my sketch above, taken to their extreme logical outcomes, liberalism and cultural nationalism seem inherently incompatible. But in fact what characterizes Schiller and subsequent German Romantics and philosophers is the conviction that *Bildung*, the process of autonomous self-development, could and should occur *simultaneously* for both the individual and the political state.

This idea of a joint development of the individual and the state is baffling to the English tradition of liberalism. For, in the social contract theory of Hobbes and Locke, individuals are imagined as formed decision-making agents *before* they enter the state. Indeed it is from the consent of each individual that the state is formed. Even if one reads such social contract theory as a theory of authorization rather than as a historical hypothesis about the actual origin of the state, the same point obtains: individuals are considered formed theoretically *prior* to the political group into which they enter. British liberalism as it descends from Hobbes and Locke sees the political state as constituted to safeguard the *preexisting* rights of individuals and this conception continues into the *laissez-faire* model of the state of classical political economy. For this tradition of British liberalism, the individual and the state are, at best, pragmatic partners, and, at worst, in constant conflict.

Thus, from the perspective of English liberalism, those aspects of the German philosophical tradition that talk in positive terms about the development of the state are taken as signs that this tradition is antiliberal. But the German philosophical tradition defined by Kant and Schiller begins with the same premise as English liberalism, namely individual freedom. And that the true descendent of this German philosophical tradition is not the cultural nation but rather the liberal state is affirmed in contemporary social theory by Habermas' use of the Kantian tradition to uphold individual human rights and to provide the basis of a noncoercive democratic public sphere.

In order to clarify this issue, let us define liberalism, as is often done, as the political commitment to the freedom of the individual. Both English liberalism and Kantian philosophy can lay claim to this definition. Where the two traditions differ, however, is their understandings of what it is for the individual to be free. For Kant and his followers, including Schiller, freedom means being free to follow the universal dictates of *reason* in the form of the moral law. On the other hand, for classical British liberalism, which, in *Culture and Anarchy*, Arnold sums up and criticizes in the phrase "doing as one likes," freedom means being free to follow one's individual *desire*, whether or not it is in agreement with reason. John Stuart Mill gives the most famous voice to this type of British liberalism in *On Liberty*, and there the very test cases of freedom are precisely those in which individual private desire comes into conflict with universal standards of reason.

These different concepts of freedom entail contrasting attitudes towards the idea of development in the two traditions. British liberalism posits that being free is being able to pursue one's desires, and that the role of the state therefore is to politically safeguard these pursuits of the individual. Given this model, there is no intrinsic concern with development for either the individual or the state. Either the state is developed enough as a practical entity to provide such safeguarding or it is not. And since the desires of the individual are what the state is designed to protect, the state has no intrinsic role in developing the individual beyond providing it with a law-governed environment in which it can safely pursue its desires, with the sole limiting constraint that the enacting of those desires not result in injury to other individuals.

This conception of the liberal state, Hannah Arendt argues in *Lectures on Kant's Political Philosophy*, is precisely what Kant promotes in his political writings.[23] And indeed Kant reflects this conception when he describes the ideal state as one "which has not only the greatest freedom . . . but also the most precise specification and preservation of the limits of this freedom in order that it can co-exist with the freedom of others."[24] In *Perpetual Peace*, Kant argues that if the political state is properly set up with safeguards for each individual's freedom then, as Arendt puts it, "a bad man can be a good citizen in a good state" (*Lectures*, 17). In these arguments, Kant reflects Mandeville's idea that private vices result in public virtues. For, as Arendt explains, Kant holds the idea that nature has a providential design for the progress of the human species as a whole that is worked out through the unfettered movements of individuals following their own desires. In his political writings, Kant does not posit a developmental role for the political state beyond its allowing nature to work out its secret designs.

But, as Arendt points out, this account of human progress in his political writings contradicts Kant's account of human morality in his philosophical works: "Infinite Progress is the law of the human species; at the same time, man's dignity demands that he be seen (every single one of us) in his particularity and, as such, be seen . . . as reflecting mankind in general. In other words, the very idea of progress . . . contradicts Kant's notion of man's dignity" (*Lectures*, 77). In Kant, the contradiction is between what each individual is ideally, that is, a rational being who wills the dictates of the moral law, and what each individual is in reality, a physically determined creature who is under the compulsion of nature in his actions. The problem is how to develop the real into the ideal. Kant does not solve this problem because it is not clear how nature, which for him is behind human progress, can transcend nature. And furthermore Kant's account of progress focuses on the species as a whole, not on the individual.[25]

Schiller seeks to find a way for actually existing human individuals to progress towards the ideal ethical state described in Kant's moral philosophy. And it is in this context that Schiller promotes the idea of the reciprocal development of the individual and the state. For if, as the Kantian model posits, ideal freedom for the individual consists in realizing and then conforming to the universal dictates of reason and ethical behavior, then there is room for development for both the individual and the state as they actually exist. For according to this idea, the *laissez-faire* state of British liberalism is only doing half its job. It is protecting individuals from being victimized by other individuals, but it is not providing an environment in which individuals can cultivate themselves to the point that they can willingly enter into the dictates of the moral law. Like Raymond Williams' definition of cultivation, Schiller's *Bildung* is something that happens in the mind of each individual, but it requires a collective effort to bring it about.

It is at this point that we can appreciate the meaningful ambiguity of the term *state*, as describing both the state of mind of the individual, and the collective body of the political state.[26] In Schillerian *Bildung*, the individual state of mind is cultivated by the collective body, and vice versa. (This same pattern of the dialectical relationship between individual and universal is seen in Coleridge's account of the symbol, as we will discuss in the next chapter.) And it should also be noted that Schiller uses *state* in its collective sense in a broader sense than what we now associate with the term *political state*. Schiller's ideal of the political state is not a totalizing one. It is neither like the paternalistic states of the German kingdoms of his time nor the totalitarian states of ours. His ideal of the political state is based on the model of the free civic engagement of individuals in the polis of ancient Greece.[27] But, as we will discuss in chapter 3 below, Schiller is notoriously vague about the form this would take in the modern era.

The ideal of a state that would develop the moral perfection of its citizens has, of course, a long tradition in western thought, beginning with Plato's *Republic*. And while the idea of twin development of individual and state is not unknown in English thought, there are perhaps historical reasons why the connection between individual and state self-development comes more easily to German philosophers at the beginning of the nineteenth century than to the English. I have described the traditional contrast between a politically unified Britain and a politically fragmented Germany in the early nineteenth century. And while I agree with recent scholarship that has questioned the necessary consequences of this difference for the question of nationalism in the two countries, this difference does remain relevant to the emphasis one finds on the development of a rational state in German political philosophy. For German philosophers, the arbitrary political demarcations of the German-speaking peoples and corresponding hodgepodge of differing political constitutions and legal practices could not help but stand in contrast with their ideals of a rational political state. Furthermore, German political fragmentation was part of a larger sense of Germany's political and cultural backwardness as compared to England and France.[28] It is this feeling of backwardness that encourages such German figures as Schiller, Novalis, and Friedrich Schlegel to call for the mutual development of both the individual and the political state, and to see these mutual developments as harmonious, rather than as conflicting, processes. In their view, neither the individual citizens nor the states, considered either politically or culturally, had yet achieved proper rationality and thus complete identity. Both were still considered to be works in progress.

PUBLIC AND PRIVATE SPHERES

Cultural nationalism has no problems defining the ideal relationship between culture and the state, but liberalism does. As I have shown, according to the theory of cultural nationalism all aspects of culture are or should be part of a common culture, which, by definition, provides the basis of unity for the nation. But for liberalism, culture becomes a problematic term that can be assimilated either to public reason or individual desire. Liberalism, in both the British and Kantian forms I have described here, has to place culture according to its dual orientation towards preserving the autonomy of the individual and preserving the unity of the political state, without which the state would not have the power to preserve individual freedom. Such a dual orientation is the basis for an essential feature of liberalism, the separation between the public and private spheres. And since for both British and Kantian liberalism, culture is not, as it is in cultural nationalism, coextensive with the cultural and political state, the problem of culture for liberalism is how to place culture in relation to the public and private spheres. To draw the contrast as sharply as possible, one can say that for the tradition of liberalism epitomized by Mill's *On Liberty*, culture should not matter in the public sphere and should be seen as purely an individual matter within the private sphere. On the other hand, for the Kantian tradition, culture only matters insofar as it can be connected to universal reason and thereby assist in the public sphere.

British liberalism, freedom as the pursuit of individual desires, has therefore been regarded as resulting in a "procedural" model of the state, with a corresponding sharp division between private culture and public procedural reason. Bentham, with his well-known lack of interest in culture, is the prime example of such a position in classical liberalism. But one can be very sympathetic to culture and still end up with the same division, as we can see in the cases of Mill and his theoretical descendent Richard Rorty. Both thinkers have argued for the value of culture, but in terms that preserve the separation of the public and the private spheres. Rorty's defense of the modern liberal state is based on the separation between the public procedural apparatus of the state and what Rorty calls "private searches for perfection."[29]

Such a separation is what antiliberal theorists, including cultural nationalists, have in mind when they critique the limits of the purely procedural liberal state. What critics of the procedural liberal state point out is that it is impossible to relegate the issue of culture to the private sphere. They argue that the issue of culture inevitably becomes an issue for the state because citizens need some shared *basis of sensibility* to ensure public consensus in the public sphere.

It is on this point that Kantian liberal theorists agree with cultural nationalists that there needs to be some shared basis of sensibility among citizens to insure the public consensus which is at the heart of the democratic liberal state. However, the Kantian liberal theorist differs with the cultural nationalist over how extensive that basis of shared sensibility needs to be. In cultural nationalism, the extension of sensibility is at every point, with the result that one can properly only speak of one sensibility embodied in a people, rather than separate people connected by shared sensibilities. The Kantian liberal theorist needs enough shared sensibility for there to be consensus, but not so much that individual autonomy is annulled. Furthermore, the Kantian liberal has a different view of the basis of shared sensibility. It should rest on *shared universal rationality* rather than on shared historically based cultural practice, as it does for the cultural nationalist.

Schiller, Coleridge, and Arnold share the Kantian liberal premise that a rational sensibility of the people is essential to the development and unity of the state, but they go beyond Kant in arguing that the aesthetic sphere is the essential medium for overcoming liberalism's problem of the separation between the public and private spheres. In their formulations of aesthetic statism, the aesthetic sphere has to act both as the basis of unifying people through the universality of reason and as the means of preserving their national cultural and individual differences. In short, it has to reconcile the universal and the particular. The means by which this reconciliation is to be achieved is through the special example and logic of the symbol, to which I now turn.

CHAPTER 2

The symbol and the aesthetic sphere

THE LITERARY SYMBOL

In literary criticism of the twentieth century the symbol has been a dominant concept. New Criticism emphasized the literary symbol, and identified it with the dual qualities of *uniqueness of expression* and *multiplicity of meaning*. The literary symbol's form was supposed to be uniquely fitted to its content, and its meanings were supposed to be never fully captured or exhausted by substitution or paraphrase.[1] In both English-language and continental literary criticism and theory there has been a strong reaction against the former hegemony and grandiose claims of critical methods based on the symbol. A defining moment in this reaction was Walter Benjamin's attempt to argue for the value of allegory in the face of the hegemony of the symbol:

For over a hundred years the philosophy of art has been subject to the tyranny of a usurper who came to power in the chaos which followed in the wake of romanticism. The striving on the part of the romantic aestheticians after a resplendent but ultimately non-committal knowledge of the absolute has secured a place in the most elementary theoretical debates about art for a notion of the symbol which has nothing more than the name in common with the genuine notion. This latter, which is the one used in the field of theology, could never have shed that sentimental twilight over the philosophy of beauty which has become more and more impenetrable since the end of early romanticism.[2]

Following Benjamin, instead of a critical method based on the symbol and the unity of the literary work, Deconstruction and other contemporary theories stressed allegory and fragmentation.[3] However, in many cases, the privileging of fragmentation in contemporary theory was no less grandiose and no less theoretically uninterrogated than the previous critical hegemony of unity and the symbol. What has been mostly missing in the pendulum swings of critical trends regarding the symbol is something that was present in Benjamin's original critique, namely, an awareness of the larger intellectual historical context out of which it emerged, and out of which its dialectical logic once made sense. The symbol, which now seems to us as an essentially aesthetic concept, in fact originally emerged out of philosophic and theological discourses responding to the crises of modernity. And indeed this extra-aesthetic origin accounts for the central role the symbol plays for those theories, like aesthetic statism, that seek an essential connection between the aesthetic and the political spheres.

THE PHILOSOPHICAL BACKGROUND OF THE SYMBOL

As we have seen, the central focus of the discourse of modernity is the issue of subjectivity, which in turn is tied to the problem of the particular and the universal. According to the Kantian tradition of modernity, the modern subject has its origin in its emancipation from the totalizing systems that had previously held it in bondage. Given that the origin of modern subjectivity is defined in terms of liberation from collectivity, what then is or should be the relationship between the individual and the collectivity? In philosophical terms, how should the particular stand in relation to the universal? How can the particular retain its identity in the face of the universal?

In trying to designate the relationship between universal and particular, there is a danger involved with privileging either term at the expense of the other. To privilege the particular can result in arid empiricism and atomized isolated subjectivity. This is the danger of liberalism. To privilege the universal can result in abstracted idealism and an absorptive annihilation of individual subjectivity by the collective. This is the danger of cultural nationalism. But what if one wants to avoid justifying one term at the expense of the other? What if one wants to assert simultaneously the reality of the universal and the particular? To do this, one has to describe a dynamic relationship between both terms, not dissolve one into the other. In short, one has to describe their *dialectical* relationship. In the tradition of dialectical theory, attempts to describe this relationship therefore inevitably lead to some version of the symbol.[4] In dialectical theory, symbols are concrete universals that both illustrate and embody the true dialectical relationship between universal and particular.

In seeking to do justice to both the individual and the collective, the logic of the symbol is a corrective to traditions that seek to privilege one term over the other. In the German idealist tradition, the privileging tends to be of the universal over the individual. In political terms, this means the dissolving of the individual to the collective. In the Romantic context of the domination of causal forces of nature over the individual, this is the danger that Schiller is most concerned with when he formulates his account of the corrective influence of the aesthetic sphere. And in the twentieth-century context of fascism and systematic political domination, this is also the danger taken up by Adorno and Habermas. In the English empiricist tradition, one has the opposite danger, namely, the dissolving of society into an aggregate of individuals. This is the central problem taken up by Coleridge, Ruskin, and Arnold, who use the logic of the symbol in order to validate the reality of such collectivities as the constitution, the family, and the state.

In the philosophical tradition, the *locus classicus* of the problem of universal and particular is Plato's discussion of the participation (*methexis*) of individual particulars in the universal *Ideas* (*eide*, traditionally translated as *the forms*). In his account of the relationship between universal and particular, Plato privileged the permanence and reality of these universal *Ideas* over their transitory instantiations in the world as empirical particulars. For Plato, empirical particulars are mere reflections of the more real *Ideas*. This view leads to his well-known criticism of art as merely a reflection of a reflection. In contrast to Platonic Idealism, the philosophical tradition of British Empiricism takes the opposite position of viewing the empirical particular as the primary component of reality. For empiricism, universal ideas are not actually existing entities but rather are "general terms," psychological and linguistic categories that result from the process of abstracting common features from the world of individual objects.

At the time of Romanticism, German Idealism attempted to synthesize the dialectical opposition between Platonic Idealism and empiricism. In Germany, Hegel stands as the most influential philosopher to make this attempt.[5] In England, drawing on many of the same influences, Coleridge independently attempted a similar philosophical synthesis.[6] In opposition to empiricism, both Hegel and Coleridge asserted the ontological reality of universal ideas. Hegel called them *Begriffe* (concepts) and Coleridge called them Ideas of Reason (as opposed to the mere ideas of the Understanding). But instead of Plato's static set of universal forms set up in heaven, Hegel and Coleridge posited universal ideas that were dynamic constitutive forces in the world. Coleridge, for example, argues that all material things develop into particular entities because of the force of these universal Ideas. And indeed, for Coleridge,

"Ideas" and "Natural Laws" are only different aspects of the same thing: "That which, contemplated *objectively* (*i.e.* as existing *externally* to the mind), we call a LAW; the same contemplated *subjectively* (*i.e.* as existing in a subject or mine) is an idea" (*C&S*, 13).[7]

While Hegel and Coleridge both describe a dialectical relationship between universal idea and particular instantiation, for reasons too complicated to enter into here, Hegel does not emphasize the symbol as a central element in his mature philosophical system.[8] Coleridge, on the other hand, both emphasizes the symbol as an essential element of his dialectical thinking and connects the symbol to the imagination and the aesthetic sphere. For this reason I will use Coleridge's account in *The Statesman's Manual* as a paradigm for explicating the origins and dialectical logic of the symbol.

Coleridge's account of the symbol in *The Statesman's Manual* is expressed in philosophical terms as a dialectical reconciliation between universal idea and particular instantiation. In this essay, as indeed in all of his later philosophical prose, Coleridge criticizes the limitations of empiricism, the dominant philosophical tradition in England, and argues for the crucial distinction between the faculties of "Reason" and "Understanding," which he models after Kant's distinction between *Vernunft* and *Verstand*.[9] According to Coleridge's account of this distinction, the understanding can only comprehend ideas in the way that empiricism defines them, that is to say, as general terms, as abstractions from the particulars of sense impressions. For Coleridge, the worldview of empiricism is an "idea-less philosophy" because it cannot comprehend the real nature of "Ideas." In contrast, a worldview informed by the faculty of reason is able to see that "Ideas" are forces that constitute and guide the material world.

This critique of the limited perspective of empiricism is the philosophical context behind Coleridge's distinction between allegory and symbol. Coleridge criticizes allegory for being "but a translation of abstract notions into a picture-language which is itself nothing but an abstraction from objects of the senses" (*SM*, 30). His criticism echoes Plato's critique of art as a mere reflection of a reflection when he charges that allegory is "unsubstantial" and that the abstraction which allegory represents is "shapeless to boot" (*SM*, 30).

But unlike Plato, Coleridge wants to defend art and the imagination. Coleridge's purpose in describing and criticizing allegory is not to denounce art as a whole, but rather is to illustrate how the limited worldview of empiricism is unable to comprehend the truth embodied in symbols and the role of the imagination in producing it. For, Coleridge asserts that the truth of the symbol is grounded by the "modifying or co-adunating" faculty of the imagination ("the faculty that makes many into one").[10] Coleridge holds up the imagination as the mediator between the material world of the senses and the world of ideas apprehended by reason. The imagination joins these two worlds through symbols. This, as we will see, is the same model of mediation and connection that Schiller attributes to the aesthetic sphere. Thus Coleridge describes the symbolic contents of the Bible as "the living *educts* of the Imagination," and describes the imagination as "that reconciling and mediatory power, which incorporates the Reason in Images of the Sense, and organizing (as it were) the flux of the Senses by the permanence and self-circling energies of the Reason, gives birth to a system of symbols, harmonious in themselves, and consubstantial with the truths, of which they are the *conductors*" (SM, 29). For Coleridge, symbols thus both embody the physical particular, and express the universal idea at the same time; they "enunciate the whole," as he memorably phrases it.

THE THEOLOGICAL BACKGROUND OF THE SYMBOL

The philosophical problem of universal and particular is thus a central context out of which the concept of the symbol develops. The other major context that propels the development of the symbol is the challenge of modernity to traditional religious doctrine. In the area of religion, the emergence of the modern autonomous subject is mostly identified with the development of enlightenment attacks on the worldview of traditional religion.[11] But there also existed thinkers, most of whom are associated with Romanticism, who, while celebrating autonomous modern subjectivity, sought to salvage the role of religion. For these thinkers, who sought to defend a notion of religion using the philosophical concepts of modernity, two approaches were possible. The first approach was to postulate the development of *new* religions, which would be based on art. New religions based on art would escape the division between thought and feeling characteristic of the crisis of modernity, because such art-religions would be based on the unity between universal idea and sensual object that is unique to art. Proposals of this sort were made by the young Hegel, Hölderlin, Schelling, and Friedrich Schlegel.[12] As we will see, Schiller's project in the *Aesthetic Letters* is a version of this argument applied to the political state.

The second approach, which can broadly be identified with the Higher Biblical Criticism, sought to uphold traditional Christianity. It sought to defend the truth value of the Bible, but instead of defending that truth in terms of literal historical accuracy, it turned instead to philosophical and metaphorical interpretations of the Bible to argue for the continuing relevance of traditional religious practices and symbols.[13] Both Coleridge and Hegel contributed to this second approach.[14] Both of these thinkers focused on the prologue to the Gospel of John, particularly the incarnation of the *logos* (the "Word"), as the key to both Christian hermeneutics and the philosophical dialectic between universal and particular. As Hegel argues in the section on "The Revealed Religion" in the *Phenomenology of Spirit* (1807), the importance of Christian myth as a development in world history is that Christ is a symbol of the union of *für-sich-sein* (*being-for-self*, individual consciousness) and *in-sich-sein* (*being-in-itself*, universal encompassing *Spirit*). For Hegel, Christ symbolizes the union of the individual and the universal, the most concrete and material (a flesh and blood man) and the most universal and abstract (God as *Spirit*). Christ as a symbol and the Incarnation as an act provide the model in which empirical particular and universal idea are combined: Christ stands for both historical particular (the historical Jesus) and divine idea (*logos*), and both of these are united in the unique act of the Incarnation. We can see this same theological account of the symbol behind Coleridge's assertion in *The Statesman's Manual* that "in the Scriptures . . . both Facts and Persons must of necessity have a two-fold significance . . . a particular and a universal application. They must be at once Portraits and Ideas" (*SM*, 30).

The fusion of universal and particular in the symbol thus reflects the model of the Incarnation, and this is also what informs Coleridge's account of the "translucencies" of the symbol. The "translucencies" sentences are now the most well-known parts of Coleridge's account of the symbol, because they are the focus of Paul de Man's brief but influential critique of the Coleridgean symbol in "The Rhetoric of Temporality." But despite this prominence, critics have not closely examined the particular dialectical logic expressed by this puzzling formula: "a Symbol . . . is characterized by a translucence of the Special in the Individual or of the General in the Especial or of the Universal in the General. Above all by the translucence of the Eternal through and in the Temporal" (*SM*, 30). The purpose of Coleridge's juxtaposition of these similar pairings is to break down empiricism's opposition between individual and general terms. A diagram will help illustrate the pattern of transposition by which Coleridge's sentence links the three sets of terms together. The first term of the first pair becomes the second term of the second pair, and the first term of the second pair becomes the second term of the third:

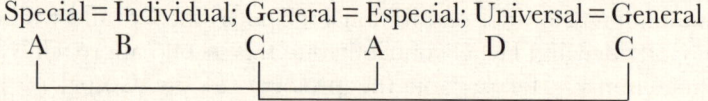

Beginning with the first pair, "Special in the Individual," "Special" stands for the universal term, the spiritual significance proclaimed by each "individual" biblical event or person. The same pattern emerges in the second pair, "General in the Especial." Here the first term is again the universal one, and the second the particular, but, by playing on the phonetic similarities between "Especial" and "Special," and by thus setting up an identity between them, even though they ostensibly occupy opposite positions in the individual/general duality, Coleridge challenges the usual duality by joining the two terms in the symbol. The last pair, "Universal in the General," is a more complicated case. Again, the first term is the universal one, but the second term, "General," is not a word that one would normally apply to the particular. Here, Coleridge is playing with the use of the word "general" by the empiricist, for whom the general term is no more than an aggregate abstraction from particulars. For Coleridge, "general" understood in such a limited sense is really a term denoting individuality. And Coleridge's whole point is that the double meaning of "general," as both universal and particular, is only a problem to those, like the empiricist, who seek to maintain a rigid opposition between particulars and universals in the first place. I will discuss the significance of the "Eternal/Temporal" pairing in the next section.

THE AUTONOMY OF THE SYMBOL

In the twentieth century, even among those who have some awareness of the philosophical and theological origins of the symbol, there has been a misrepresentation of the political consequences of using the symbol as the basis for political theory. For many theorists of this century, the political use of the symbol represents the worst sort of totalizing ideology. Thus, Adorno notes ironically in his discussion of the totalizing style of the products of the culture industry in *Dialectic of*

Enlightenment that "The whole and the parts are alike; there is no antithesis and no connection. Their prearranged harmony is a mockery of what had to be striven after in the great bourgeois works of art" (*DE*, 126). If one understands the logic of the symbol as the elimination of individuality within a dominant whole, then it becomes the model for the totalitarian politics of fascism and state communism of the twentieth century. This is the situation that Adorno sees in almost every aspect of the contemporary world, in which individuals are reduced to complete copies of prefabricated "universals." But, significantly, the one place in the contemporary world where this is not the case for Adorno is the aesthetic sphere. And this is because, despite Adorno's rejection of the aesthetic tradition of the symbol, in Adorno's own aesthetic theory he carries on a central element of that tradition, aesthetic autonomy, as I will discuss in the final chapter.

Because of the influence of Benjamin and Adorno in contemporary theory, the tradition of the symbol has been identified with the annihilation of individualism. But this was not the way that the logic of the symbol was expressed by those theorists like Coleridge and Schiller who sought to use it as the basis of political theory. For Schiller, the autonomy of the aesthetic sphere is the basis by which the freedom of the individual will be formed and preserved.[15] For Coleridge, the autonomy of the symbol expresses the autonomy of subjectivity itself. In their formulations, the freedom of the individual is an intrinsic part of the dialectical logic of the symbol. For, in order to *represent*, that is, to *stand for*, the symbol must also *stand apart*, that is, retain a distinct particular identity in the face of the universal concept it represents. This simultaneous standing for and standing apart is what I will call the logic of the symbol. The symbol must be both a real particular and stand for the universal concept. It thus embodies the reconciliation of universal and particular, but it only does so by keeping some element of distance, of removal from that which it represents. If the symbol had no distinction from the universal concept it represented, if it participated completely in the universal, then it would be completely absorbed and lose its identity as a real particular.

This element of subjective autonomy is illustrated by the fourth translucency pair of Coleridge's definition of the symbol, "the Eternal through and in the Temporal." This follows the same pattern as the first three pairings, with the universal term in the first position, and the particular term in the second. But the fourth pairing incorporates the element of time and allows us to view the movement through the first three translucencies as a narrative of providential history in which particulars, here the particular human agents of biblical history, act in harmony with the universal, namely God's providential design. This view is expressed more fully in a later passage in *The Statesman's Manual*:

In the Bible every agent appears and acts as a self-subsisting individual: each has a life of its own, and yet all are one life. The elements of necessity and free-will are reconciled in the higher power of an omnipresent Providence, that predestinates the whole in the moral freedom of the integral parts. Of this the Bible never suffers us to lose sight. The root is never detached from the ground. *SM*, 31-2

This is Coleridge's account of the Hebrew people in terms of a dialectical reconciliation of individual and universal. In this account, Coleridge, like Schiller in the *Aesthetic Letters*, seeks to reconcile the causal necessity of history with Kant's moral freedom of the autonomous subject. Coleridge's view of providence is human freedom working with, not supplanted by, God's design, an individuality grounded in, not opposed to or obliterated by, collectivity. This is the social and political dimension of his claim that the symbol retains the particular, even in its complete participation in the universal.

THE SYMBOL AND THE AESTHETIC SPHERE

Following Coleridge, I have defined the symbol as an individual embodiment of the dialectical reconciliation of universal and particular. Schiller defines the aesthetic sphere as the sphere in which such a reconciliation occurs, or, more precisely, is perceived to occur by the subject. In this sense, the terms *symbol* and *aesthetic sphere* are closely related. But one should note the difference between a *model* of reconciliation and a *medium* of reconciliation here, because this is a distinction that bears on the effect the aesthetic work or sphere can be claimed to have on the social world. Albrecht Wellmer highlights this distinction in a critique of Adorno's aesthetic theory.[16] For, even if one grants that some things like Coleridge's symbols or Adorno's works of art manage to obtain a dialectical reconciliation between universal and particular, the question remains of how these things help individual human beings and human society as a whole achieve the same reconciled situation. The mere existence of dialectically reconciled entities does not, on its own, provide a means through which human beings or human society can achieve the same form of reconciliation.[17]

Such a critique is particularly piercing to an aesthetic theory like Adorno's that stresses the separate existence of works of art as objective entities in their own right. But, for the theorists of aesthetic statism, the autonomy of the aesthetic sphere is not based on the separate existence of artistic works, but, rather, the autonomy of the aesthetic sphere is based on the autonomy of human subjectivity itself. This is particularly emphasized in Schiller's account of an aesthetic *education*. For Schiller, because aesthetic works are expressions of human subjectivity, they provide a medium, a place of contemplation, the aesthetic sphere, through which all human beings can seek the freedom that art embodies and achieves through its reconciliations of objective and subjective, and universal and particular. In this sense, the aesthetic sphere itself stands as a symbol of the reconciliation that could or should also obtain in the everyday world. In contrast to Adorno's aesthetic theory, for Schiller, the aesthetic sphere is thus essentially and inseparably connected to the human world through the element of human subjectivity.

But Schiller does stress the autonomy of the aesthetic sphere from the demands of the mundane world. This is another way in which the aesthetic sphere reflects the logic of the symbol. As we saw, the symbol can only be representative (stand for) if it is also autonomous (stands apart) to some degree. In the same way, the aesthetic sphere is only able to function as a symbol of the reconciliation of subject and object for the mundane world as long as the aesthetic sphere retains some degree of separation from the mundane world.

Among the theorists of aesthetic statism, this logic of being both crucially guiding and also somewhat removed is particularly expressed in Arnold's account of the relationship between culture and society. Against his critics who condemn the value of culture by questioning its immediate impact on the pressing political issues of the day, Arnold turns the issue on its head. Culture is to be valued precisely because it is removed from the world of immediate decision making. Because culture is outside of the immediate causal nexus of the world, it allows for the cultivation of a perspective that can be more complete than one formed for the sake of a particular pragmatic purpose. This more complete perspective will in time influence the very categories of the everyday world.

This logic is taken to its most extreme degree in Adorno, for whom the philosophical and political value of the aesthetic work resides in its objective otherness. For Adorno, this objective otherness allows the artwork to escape from the totalizing web of reason of the administered world. But as Wellmer's critique points up and as I will discuss in the final chapter, it also creates the problem of how such radically autonomous works can be a means of guidance to the mass of humanity caught in the web of totalizing reason.

CHAPTER 3

Schiller's aesthetic state

THE POLITICS OF AESTHETIC AUTONOMY

As I have noted, many critics have cast the shadow of twentieth-century German National Socialism back into the previous centuries when they have assessed German political philosophy. This is particularly true of Schiller, whose idea of the aesthetic state has been charged with laying the groundwork for twentieth-century German fascism either directly, by presenting a totalizing political ideology under the guise of the aesthetic, or indirectly, by promoting an escapist aesthetic ideology of politics among German intellectuals that thus blinded them to the signs of danger in the world of *Realpolitik*. A version of this first kind of criticism is evident in Paul de Man's essay "Aesthetic Formalization: Kleist's *Über das Marionettentheater*," in which de Man criticizes Schiller for promoting an "ideology of the aesthetic" behind which hides "a principle of formalization rigorous enough to produce its own codes and systems of inscription" which "functions as a restrictive coercion that allows only for the reproduction of its own system, at the exclusion of all others."[1] To the familiar shadow of Nazi totalitarianism, de Man thus adds the specter of linguistic totalization. But he does not discuss the specifics of Schiller's project in the *Aesthetic Letters* in this essay, and, furthermore, the terms by which de Man defines the danger of Schiller's work are general enough to indite any attempt at systematic philosophy.

De Man discusses Schiller more directly and extensively in the transcribed lecture "Kant and Schiller," in which he charges Schiller with having psychologized and thus having distorted the philosophical project of Kant.[2] The bulk of the lecture remains at a very abstract level of theoretical critique, but de Man does briefly argue that the *Aesthetic Letters* are the origin of cultural nationalism because it is "the basis of concepts such as 'culture,' and the thought that it is possible to move from individual works of art to a collective, massive notion of art, which would be, for example, one of national characteristics, and which would be the culture of a nation, of a general, social dimension called 'cultural'" (*Aesthetic Ideology*, 150). But, once again, de Man does not substantiate this argument by referring to the specifics of the *Aesthetic Letters*. He concludes the lecture with a passage from Joseph Goebbels that compares the statesman to an artist who forms his people as a work of art.[3] While admitting that the Goebbels quote "is a grievous misreading of Schiller's aesthetic state," de Man goes on to add that "the principle of this misreading does not essentially differ from the misreading which Schiller inflicted on his own predecessor – namely, Kant" (155). In contrast to this view, in this chapter I will indicate the very ways in which Schiller carried on the central goals of Kant's liberalism. But beyond the inaccuracy of de Man's point, I must also censure the intellectually dishonest way in which, instead of actually engaging in an analysis that would substantiate this charge, de Man merely evokes the prejudicial background tradition of connecting Schiller and Nazism. Without wishing to engage in *ad hominem* arguments, I will simply point out the back-handed way in which de Man is insinuating an equivalence between Schiller and Goebbels, and leave it to individual readers to draw whatever irony they might find in the fact that it is Paul de Man making such a charge.

Without evoking the shadow of National Socialism, Martha Woodmansee has recently raised the main issues behind the second traditional critique of Schiller, namely, that Schiller's aesthetic state represents an ideology of retreat from real political engagement. In *The Author, Art, and the Market: Rereading the History of Aesthetics*, Woodmansee mounts an important critique on the concept of aesthetic autonomy, which she sees as the central premise of aesthetics from Kant and Schiller down to the present.[4] Woodmansee traces the origin of aesthetic autonomy to *Towards a Unification of all the Fine Arts and Letters under the Concept of Self-Sufficiency* (1785) by Karl Philipp Moritz (1756–93), published five years before the publication of Kant's *Critique of Judgement*. In his treatise, Moritz defines works of art as "'self-sufficient totalities' produced simply to be contemplated 'for their own sake' – that is 'disinterestedly'" (Woodmansee, *Author, Art*, 11). In attempting to historically contextualize the emergence of this concept of aesthetic autonomy, Woodmansee discusses the expansion of the market for popular literature. Moritz was a prolific writer whose most ambitious philosophic works were never appreciated by the public, and Woodmansee argues that "by shifting the measure of a work's value from its pleasurable effect on the audience to such purely intrinsic considerations as 'the perfection of the work itself,' Moritz arms his own and all difficult writing against the eventuality of a hostile or indifferent reception" (*Author, Art*, 32). Woodmansee applies the same interpretation to Schiller and the *Aesthetic Letters*, likewise arguing that Schiller felt rejected by the mass public and thus formulated his account of an autonomous aesthetic sphere as an ego-saving strategy. She thus portrays an elitist and antipopulist Schiller who stresses the autonomy of the artwork for his own benefit and who opposes what she terms an "instrumentalist" account of poetry, namely the idea that poetry has a goal and that is to "move" the audience. She champions Gottfried August Bürger (author of the popular supernatural poem *Lenore*) as a preferred example of poetic populism, and endorses his Herder-like pronouncements on basing poetry on the language of the people and connecting it to traditional national epics.

Because she views Schiller's account of the aesthetic as a retreat and defense against the demands of the market, Woodmansee also calls into doubt the professed political ends of the aesthetic sphere expressed in the *Aesthetic Letters*. This brings up in a new light a long-standing ambiguity in the interpretation of this work. The question is whether Schiller presents two contradictory arguments for the purpose of the aesthetic sphere. Is its purpose to lead to the creation of the ideal political state, or is the aesthetic state to be pursued as an end in itself?[5] Woodmansee's critique thus raises two main charges: (1) that Schiller's argument for the aesthetic sphere is elitist and undermines individual autonomy since it denies the validity of individual subjective judgments of art; and (2) that despite his pretensions, the project of the *Aesthetic Letters* is not really political. I will challenge the basis of both of Woodmansee's major criticisms, but I should say at the outset that my goal in doing so is not to mount a wholesale defense of Schiller's aesthetic theory. As I will argue in my final chapter, because Schiller's theory of the aesthetic sphere is based on the metaphysically privileged model of the symbol, it is no longer a viable option for contemporary theory. But while Schiller's solution to the problem of the conflict between the subjective and objective existence of the individual in relation to the political state is one we can no longer claim, his formulation of the problem continues to be important. In terms of contemporary theory, Schiller's formulation of the public nature of aesthetic experience provides an important framework through which we can understand and assess Habermas' theories of the public sphere and communicative action.

Woodmansee raises the crucial issue of how to view the origin of the aesthetic sphere in history, and I support her project of scrutinizing the central premises of aesthetic theory by holding them up to the particulars of material history. I would also argue, however, that one may well concede the very personal motivations that Woodmansee presents of Moritz and Schiller as struggling writers but also take the position that personal motivation is not the sole or even the primary horizon of meaning for a cultural development as far-reaching as the development of the modern concept of aesthetic autonomy. For, despite Woodmansee's professed intentions to discuss the origin of the concept of the aesthetic sphere as "rooted in the far-reaching changes in the production, distribution, and consumption of reading material that marked the later eighteenth century" (*Author, Art,* 32), her focus on the personal motivations of Moritz and Schiller seems to reduce the origin of modern aesthetics to a case of sour grapes on the part of individual writers. The point that is implicit in Woodmansee's analysis of the material conditions of the later eighteenth century but gets lost in the emphasis on personal motivation is the *inevitability* of the development of a concept of the aesthetic given the effects the democratization of culture has on the relationship between author and audience. Once the audience ceases to be an audience of near peers, as presupposed in Renaissance and neoclassical models of rhetoric, and becomes a heterogeneous mass reading public, the assured correspondence between rhetorical forms and audience reaction is also lost. This lack of any ground for literary taste beyond the market is one of the central developments of modernity, and the point is that, then as now, this was seen as a hugely problematic development with far-reaching social and political ramifications.

Among contemporary theory, the Frankfurt school has developed the most sustained analysis and critique of the effects of the modern market on the creation and consumption of culture. Habermas' work is crucial here, because he does afford the market a central role in the development of the public sphere, specifically the same expanding literary market of the eighteenth century that Woodmansee points to. For Habermas, the development of the literary market plays a crucial role by opening up new forums of expression for individual subjectivity. Individuals develop their subjectivity through the expression of their taste through the new private market for the arts as entertainment (nonoccasional music) and for reflection (novels, literary journals, newspapers). In this way, the literary public sphere paves the way for the political public sphere. But, unlike Woodmansee, Habermas does not collapse the public sphere into the market. The crucial element for Habermas is the *autonomy* of the public sphere based on a concept of rationality that is ultimately independent from the market. Without this notion of autonomy there is no way to distinguish between situations in which the market serves to develop preexisting subjectivity, as Habermas argues in *Structural Transformation of the Public Sphere* is the case in the early bourgeois public sphere, and situations in which the market dictates tastes to consumers, as Horkheimer and Adorno argue in *Dialectic of Enlightenment* is the case in the twentieth-century "culture industry."

The irony of Woodmansee's critique of Schiller is that she seeks to cast him within a formalist, antihumanist, strain of aesthetics.[6] But Schiller's account of the aesthetic is explicitly expressed in the service of promoting humanism, specifically a Kantian model of individual self-determination. The whole purpose of Schiller's account of the aesthetic education is not to deny individual subjectivity, but to develop it. Schiller saw modern subjectivity as being in a process of development, and he argues that it is precisely through the autonomy of the aesthetic sphere that the individual could develop into full and free subjectivity. According to Schiller's argument, the aesthetic sphere has to be autonomous, that is free from outside constraints, so that individual subjectivity can achieve the same free state. Certainly, there are valid objections that can be brought against Schiller's account of an autonomous aesthetic sphere, but it is important to acknowledge that the purpose of positing such an aesthetic sphere is to grant freedom to the subject, not, as Woodmansee argues, to take freedom away from the subject by placing all autonomy in the work of art. In order to understand Schiller's project of aesthetic statism, it is important to see how aesthetic autonomy in Schiller plays the same role as the autonomy of the public sphere for Habermas, that is, of promoting the autonomy of the subject.

THE PROJECT OF THE ''AESTHETIC LETTERS''

For Schiller, at the heart of the crisis of modernity is the fragmentation of the mental faculties of the subject. This fragmentation is for him a result of the division of labor brought on by the advance of material civilization. This advance in civilization leads to an increased industrial efficiency and a general increase in the standard of living. But it also produces a modern political situation in which the political state can no longer be represented by any single human being, as was the case, Schiller argues, in the ancient Greek polis. According to Schiller, in modern times humanity is now divided between the lower classes ruled by "crude, lawless instincts" (*AL*, v.4) and the cultivated classes who present a "repugnant spectacle of lethargy" (*AL*, v.5). Both these classes have lost their human freedom and are ruled by forces outside of themselves, the lower classes by basic material drives and needs, the cultivated classes by new dependencies created by civilization itself: "Civilization, far from setting us free, in fact creates some new need with every new power it develops in us. The fetters of the physical tighten ever more alarmingly . . ." (*AL*, v.5). For Schiller, the wholeness of human nature must be restored before political reform can take place: "we must continue to regard every attempt at political reform as untimely, and every hope based on it as chimerical, as long as the split within man is not healed, and his nature so restored to wholeness that it can itself become the artificer of the State, and guarantee the reality of this political creation of Reason" (*AL*, VII.1).

For Schiller, the crucial importance of the aesthetic work to reconciling the fragmentation of modern subjectivity is that the aesthetic work is subject to two opposing worlds. In this way, it reflects the condition of humanity itself. Carrying over the Kantian distinction between the phenomenal and noumenal aspects of the self, Schiller describes these two aspects as "Condition" (*Zustand*) and "Person" (*Person*). The human being is part of the physical world ("Condition") as a physical object subject to the laws of nature, like any physical object. But more importantly, the human being is part of the world of rationality, what he identifies with the term "Form" (*Gestalt*), and it is through this that the human being strives to be a "Person." Corresponding to these divided aspects are the two opposing attractions or "drives" that the human being feels to the two opposing worlds: the sensuous drive (*Stofftrieb*) and the formal drive (*Formtrieb*). The sensuous drive produces desires for objects in the material world. In contrast to the material orientation of the sensuous drive, the formal drive "proceeds from the absolute existence of man, or from his rational nature, and is intent on giving him the freedom to bring harmony into the diversity of his manifestations, and to affirm his Person among all the changes of Condition" (*AL*, XII.4).

Schiller states that a literal interpretation of Kant's moral philosophy can lead to viewing "material things as nothing but a obstacle, and imagining that our sensuous nature . . . must be in conflict with reason"

(*AL*, XIII.2, footnote). Opposing this puritanical understanding of Kantian morality, Schiller insists that the sensuous drive cannot simply be ignored or suppressed: "Thought may indeed escape it for the moment ... but suppressed nature soon resumes her rights, and presses for reality of existence, for some content to our knowing and some purpose for our doing" (*AL*, XII.3). Schiller thus attempts to reconcile those two aspects of the individual that Kant left in contradiction: the individual as subject to the universal laws of morality, and the individual as the pursuer of his or her own individual desires. Drawing on Fichte, Schiller describes a reciprocal action between subjectivity and the material world. He thus augments the letter of Kant's philosophy by stressing that the material world ("Condition") is necessary for leading the subject to reason, not just pure reason ("Form"). Instead of simply seeking to free ourselves from the material world, Schiller argues that, as human beings, we need to acknowledge the material world and incorporate it as an element of our subjectivity. Schiller therefore points to the need to "arm abstract form with sensuous power, lead concept back to intuition, and law back to feeling" (*AL*, XVII.4).

Now the aesthetic work is uniquely suited for reconciling the two opposing human drives because it also exhibits the same dual nature: it is a physical object in the material world (marble, sound, paint, ink, and paper); and, as an object given *form*, it is the expression of rational subjectivity. But unlike the human being in which these two aspects of "Condition" and "Form" seem in conflict, in the aesthetic work these two aspects are harmonized. This harmony is what Schiller means by "beauty" (*Schönheit*), and this harmonious beauty is what defines the aesthetic sphere.

On the analogy of the sensuous and formal drives, Schiller calls our attraction towards beauty and the aesthetic sphere the "play drive" (*Spieltrieb*), and sees in this drive a reconciliation of the other two drives. And because the aesthetic work harmonizes both drives, it can serve to help the two kinds of imbalances in human natures that arise in human beings, favoring the sensuous drive or the formal drive: "By means of beauty, sensuous man is led to form and thought; by means of beauty spiritual man is brought back to matter and restored to the world of sense" (*AL*, XVII.1). "The first of these services she renders to natural man, the second to civilized man" (*AL*, XVII.4). Following the logic of the symbol, as I discussed above in chapter 2, the aesthetic sphere is the space of freedom in which and through which the individual can reconcile what seem like the conflicting demands of the material world and the moral laws. For, in the aesthetic sphere, these two worlds do not appear to be in conflict. In the aesthetic sphere, they are experienced as harmonious.

AESTHETIC AND SUBJECTIVE AUTONOMY

Woodmansee regards Schiller's argument for the aesthetic autonomy of the work of art as seeking to suppress the free subjectivity of the viewer. This raises the question of how one defines subjectivity and freedom. Despite the left-leaning rhetoric of her critique, Woodmansee's model of subjectivity turns out to be that of British individualist liberalism, which, (as I discussed in chapter 1 above) posits the centrality of individual desire. This becomes explicit in her endorsement of the *laissez-faire* aesthetic theory of Archibald Alison and Francis Jeffrey, which, according to Woodmansee, "affirms art's complete integration into a economy in which the value of an object is a function of its utility to consumers who cannot be wrong – except by consuming too little" (*Author, Art*, 136). Woodmansee seeks to connect Jeffrey's "confidence in the free market for culture" with contemporary concerns for respecting cultural diversity, and she approvingly discusses a passage from Jeffrey in which the judgment of cockney tourists on the lack of beauty of the Highlands is granted the same validity as the opposing judgment of the upper-class viewer (*Author, Art*, 133–4).

For Woodmansee, Jeffrey's account of the relativity of perceptions of beauty is the most democratic of aesthetic doctrines. But I would argue that Jeffrey's aesthetic relativism is no more intrinsically democratic than Schiller's arguments for aesthetic autonomy are intrinsically anti-democratic. In the relationship between aesthetic and political theories, one must view theories within a specific historical context in order to accurately ascertain their actual political implications. Woodmansee's attempt to view the *laissez-faire* principles of Jeffrey as a "joyful affirmation of diversity" however illustrates a failure to do this. For there is a world of difference in the political implications of arguing for the relativity of taste when there is an equality of power among social classes and when there is a status quo of hierarchical power. Jeffrey's affirmation of diversity is not linked to any project that would give political weight to the opinions of the working class.[7] Rather it simply reinscribes on a theoretical level the practical fact of the vast differences of perception that separate social classes due to the differences in their material and social conditions. Thus what Woodmansee describes in contemporary terms as Jeffrey's affirmation of diversity is, given the political context of his day, actually the indifference of the middle-of-the-road Whig who freely grants members of the working class the relative validity of their quaint opinions precisely because their opinions do not and cannot have any political consequences given the actual economic and political structure of the state.

In order to understand the political implications of Schiller's aesthetic theory, we have to remember how different his model of free subjectivity is from that of British individualist liberalism. Schiller sees the exclusive emphasis on individual desire as ultimately destructive of human personality, and he criticizes the basis of British individualistic liberalism in his discussion of the fleeting and ultimately identity-destroying nature of "inclination" (*Neigung*): "Inclination can only say: this is good for you as an individual and for your present need; but your individuality and your present need will be swept away by change and what you now so ardently desire will one day become the object of your aversion" (*AL*, XII.4). Instead of locating individual identity in ever-changing individual desire, Schiller argues that the proper basis for a lasting identity is through following what he calls the Formal Drive, the moral feelings proceeding from the Kantian concept of the universal moral law, and thus treating "one moment of your life as if it were eternity" (*AL*, XII.5). Indeed for Schiller, it is not really an option for a human being to chose between following immediate desire (giving oneself up to material "Condition") or following the moral law. Because he sees human personhood ("Personality") composed as a union of opposing drives, one would cease to have an identity as an individual at all should one annul one of those drives altogether. One would become "self-seeking, and yet without a self" (*AL*, XXIV.2).

The analog to the ethical position that views unrestrained individualistic desire as the height of human freedom is the aesthetic position that views the essence of the work of art as its freedom from any rules. Schiller calls those who hold this aesthetic position "sensationalist aestheticians" (*sensualen Ästhetiker*), and he argues that they "entrust themselves blindly to guidance of their feeling" and "can arrive at no concept of beauty, because in the totality of their sensuous impressions of it they can distinguish no separate elements." Schiller's argument against this approach to aesthetics is that they "do not, however, reflect that the freedom in which they rightly locate the essence of beauty, is not just lawlessness but rather harmony of laws, not arbitrariness but supreme inner necessity" (*AL*, XVIII.4). We can see the parallels here between human and aesthetic autonomy for Schiller. Autonomy for both lies not in freedom from all rules, but rather in following inner rules. If the law comes from the essence of the being, it is not felt as a restraint on freedom, but rather is felt as freedom of self-development.

As I discussed in chapter 1 above, the reason that Schiller's emphasis on individual autonomy can be hard to see from the perspective of British individualism is that Schiller, following Kant, discusses the project of the simultaneous development of the individual and human beings as a species. What makes this simultaneous development possible for Schiller is the universality of reason. As I have noted, for Kant, freedom is asserting one's autonomy as a rational being. Kant includes the universal moral law (the categorical imperative) as part of rationality. For Kant, any rational being assents to the universality of reason, including the universal moral law. And thus the compulsion to follow the moral law is an inner one: it is simply doing what, in ideal conditions, one would already and always want to do.

But our condition as human beings is never ideal. We have a physical existence that limits our ability to fulfill the categorical imperatives of the moral law. The aesthetic sphere however gives us the opportunity to stand back and assert our identity as rational moral beings. Thus in *Critique of Judgement*, Kant ranks poetry first among the arts because "it lets the mind feel its ability – free, spontaneous, and independent of natural determination – to contemplate and judge phenomenal nature."[8] For Kant, one's aesthetic response (what he calls the "judgement of taste") implies a universal judgment. That is, in regarding something as beautiful, implicit in the judgment is the idea that anyone else would also freely make the same judgment, that is, find the object beautiful.

This issue of the freedom of the aesthetic response lies behind those aspects of the *Aesthetic Letters* that seem to promote a formalist aesthetics. Schiller argues that

> In a truly successful work of art the contents [*Inhalt*] should effect nothing, the form everything; for only through the form is the whole man affected, through the subject matter [*Inhalt*], by contrast only one or the other of his functions. Subject matter, then, however sublime and all-embracing it may be, always has a limiting effect upon the spirit, and it is only from form that true aesthetic freedom can be looked for. *AL*, XXII.5

Thus, we can see why many critics, most recently Woodmansee, charge Schiller with being a formalist in the modernist sense, that is, with emphasizing the aesthetic form of the artwork over its representational or affective features. But what must be remembered is that what Schiller means by "form" is the complete opposite of what the term usually means in theories of modern art. Modernist formalism focuses on the medium as sensuous expression: paintings as plays of colored paint, sculpture as masses of three-dimensional material, poetry as sound. But "form" for Schiller means the *nonphysical* aspect of the work. Schiller's form connects to the formal drive, to the guiding *rationality* of the work, not to the sensuous drive, not to the physical particulars of the medium. For Schiller, the physical particulars of the work of art, which he denotes by *Stoff*, and the subject matter, i.e. what the work represents, which he denotes by *Inhalt*, both stand opposed to Form. *Stoff* stands opposed because it is actual physical material and *Inhalt* because it represents a content which is ultimately traceable to the physical world.9

It is true that by emphasizing "form," as the rational organizing aspect of the work of art, Schiller does, like some modern formalists, give a secondary role to the representational and affective aspects of the work of art. But the important issue is why he does so. Woodmansee criticizes Schiller for moving aesthetics away from an affective model, what she calls, oddly enough given its mechanistic resonances, an "instrumentalist" account. Her argument is that, contra Kant and Schiller, art has a purpose, and that purpose is to move the audience emotionally. Now for Kant and especially Schiller, art does have a purpose, namely to develop the freedom of subjectivity. (And it is within that context that Kant uses the famous but frequently misunderstood statement that the work of art displays a "purposiveness without purpose," as I will discuss below.) But what is behind Schiller's objection to art's main purpose as eliciting an emotional response? For, he states that "the unfailing effect of beauty is a freedom from passion" (*AL*, XXII.5). Now the modernist formalist exclusively values the aesthetic form of the art object, and thus excludes from consideration the issue of the emotional effect of the work of art on the mind of the viewer. Schiller's whole project involves discussing the effect of the art object on the mind, but the effect he is interested in is different from and in a certain way antithetical to eliciting a simple emotional response.

Schiller does not object to there being an emotional component in the work of art. In discussing "arts which affect the passions, such as tragedy," Schiller does criticize them for not being "entirely free arts since they are enlisted in the service of a particular aim (that of pathos)," but he adds that "no true connoisseur of art will deny that works even of this class are the more perfect, the more they respect the freedom of the spirit even amid the most violent storms of passion" (*AL*, XXII.5). Thus what he objects to is not emotion *per se*, but that emotion should totally control one's response. Schiller's argument is based on the same idea that makes the word *manipulative* a negative term in aesthetic criticism. We criticize a work for being manipulative not simply because it seeks to stir our emotions, but because it seeks to bypass our intelligence in stirring them. Once again, even in his criticisms of affective art, Schiller's aim is to uphold the autonomy of the subject.

UNIVERSALITY, DIVERSITY, AND AESTHETIC STATISM

The universality claims of Kantian aesthetics have been viewed, especially in the current climate of valuing cultural relativity and diversity, as the basis of stifling individual freedom and of maintaining an elite and rigid cultural canon. Now, there is no question that Kant sought to uphold the idea of universality in philosophy, morality, and aesthetics and on this basis opposed cultural relativism. And there is no way that Kant's ideas can be made palatable to thoroughgoing cultural relativists. But there is something to be learned by interrogating the now commonplace view that cultural relativism is intrinsically politically progressive and that universalism is intrinsically politically conservative. What one finds in Kant and Schiller are arguments for universality presented in the service of progressive enlightenment liberalism. From the perspective of Kant's liberalism, the implicit universality of the judgment of the beautiful is not meant as a means of imposing the view of an elite cultural orthodoxy. Rather, Kant presents it as another example of the central enlightenment idea of a common basis of humanity, an idea that Kant employs in his political writings precisely in opposition to the rule of political elites.

Kant and Schiller argue for the value of the arts on the basis of how they unite, rather than, as in the case of cultural nationalism, how they distinguish and differentiate groups and individuals. What art promises for Kant, and especially Schiller, is a means of communication that both elicits a free response from the individual and serves as basis of communal agreement.[10] In a passage that particularly reverberates with Habermas' modern theory of communicative action, Schiller thus asserts: "All other forms of communication divide society, because they relate exclusively either to the private receptivity or the private proficiency of its individual members, hence to that which distinguishes man from man; only the aesthetic mode of communication unites society because it relates to that which is common to all" (*AL*, XXVII.10).

The question, however, that naturally arises for the contemporary theorist is: does not any appeal to a universality in human beings involve the imposition of a single reading of every aesthetic object and a single canon of aesthetic objects? Now, although the aesthetic theories of Kant and Schiller are predicated on a theory of universal human nature, their theories of the aesthetic do not entail the rigid uniformity of response so criticized by contemporary theory, nor do their theories dictate a priori which works will provide such an aesthetic response. One reason why contemporary theorists make the jump from the universality of the aesthetic response to a rigid notion of the canon is that they tend to identify Kant's judgment of the beautiful with modern notions of valid interpretation. But, while the two concepts have some overlap, they denote very different approaches to the question of the aesthetic.

Kant's judgment of the beautiful is based on the idea that people should find *the same things beautiful*, not that they should necessarily find *the exact same meanings* in those beautiful things. Now, of course, presumably it is out of that class of universally agreed-upon beautiful works that critics would focus on in discussions of meaning. But, Kant and Schiller have very little to say about interpretation and meaning in the sense that contemporary theory has defined it. Indeed, for Kant the central quality of the aesthetic response is its ineffableness. We cannot explain the meaning of the work of art because we cannot put it under a teleological concept. We can say that it is good, but we cannot say what it is good *for*. This is what Kant means by his famous phrase "purposiveness without purpose" to describe the aesthetic object. He means that we cannot find a purpose for the work of art in the physical world, that is, a purpose relating to our existence as phenomenal beings. The purpose of the work of art relates to our existence as noumenal beings, as rational entities not limited by the causal nexus of the physical world.

As a practitioner of the arts as well as a philosophizer of them, Schiller was well aware of the many things that can be said about individual works of art. But he retains the same basic metaphysical framework as Kant, and it is crucial to his arguments for the aesthetic education that the aesthetic sphere be removed from either moral or material standards of teleology. The only extended discussion of an individual work of art in the *Aesthetic Letters* is of a statue, the Juno Ludovisi. And there the analysis serves to substantiate the Kantian idea that the work of art cannot be placed under a concept of the Understanding. Schiller describes how the statue strikes the viewer as possessing opposing qualities of beauty and sublimity, so that the viewer is struck with both feelings of attraction and repulsion. The viewer is "irresistibly moved and drawn by those former qualities, kept at a distance by these latter" with the result that "we find ourselves at one and the same time in a state of utter repose and supreme agitation, and there results that wondrous stirring of the heart for which mind has no concept nor speech any name" (*AL*, xv.9).

However, even granting the considerable differences between Kant's judgment of the beautiful and modern notions of valid interpretation, one is still left with what seems like a basic conflict between the universality of the aesthetic response as posited by Kant, and the diversity of cultural practices as posited by the cultural nationalist. It is in trying to reconcile this central conflict that Schiller goes beyond Kant and posits what I have called aesthetic statism. Like Kant, Schiller places both individual difference and the differences between cultures on the same ground, as both resulting from the contingencies of the material world and physical causation, and thus seemingly in opposition to universal reason.

However, in the same way, and on the same ground of the aesthetic sphere, that Schiller goes beyond Kant in arguing for the material world as a path rather than a mere hindrance to universal morality, so too Schiller goes beyond Kant in attempting to harmonize the conflicting concepts of universal and diverse notions of culture. For, Schiller explicitly recognizes the demands of both universality and diversity: "Reason does indeed demand unity; but Nature demands multiplicity; and both these kinds of laws make their claim upon man" (*AL*, iv.3). This statement expresses the theoretical core of aesthetic statism, the project of reconciling the universality of the moral law with the diversity among individuals and peoples created by the contingencies of nature, through an appeal to the uniquely harmonizing effect of the aesthetic sphere. Typical of the dialectical form of argument of the *Aesthetic Letters*, Schiller argues that neither universality nor diversity should be annulled by the other: "whenever Reason starts to introduce the unity of the moral law into any actually existing society she must beware of damaging the variety of Nature. And whenever Nature endeavours to maintain her variety within the moral frameworks of society, moral unity must not suffer any infringement thereby" (*AL*, iv.7).

That Schiller is trying to harmonize universality with the diversity of humankind indicates that his aesthetic theory is no mere cover for cultural elitism. It is through Schiller's attempt to reconcile these two claims that his account of the aesthetic connects to the liberal idea of an individual private sphere (as I discussed above in chapter 1), namely, that within the parameters of shared community sensibility there is freedom of latitude for individual subjectivity.[11] Furthermore, there is nothing in Schiller's aesthetic theory that defines or fixes a cultural canon along traditionalist lines.

It is actually the cultural nationalist, who, in the name of national history, has the essential stake in fixing both individual interpretation and a canon. For the cultural nationalist, a fixed canon of works and interpretations plays the essential role of codifying the national culture and providing the materials out of which the identity of the members of the cultural nation are to be formed. Schiller implicitly agrees with the cultural nationalist that the accidents of material history, the causal chain of necessity (phenomenal nature), the story of the land, is what is responsible for the differences between groups and individuals. But the difference is that Schiller argues that human identity should be formed by achieving some degree of separation between subjectivity and the causal chain of material history rather than in embracing the accidents of material determination as the sole basis of identity.

THE POLITICAL AND AESTHETIC STATE

I have explained Schiller's theory of aesthetic statism by contrasting it with the full-blown concept of cultural nationalism laid out in chapter 1 above. This explanation needs to be qualified by the historical fact that Schiller lived and wrote before such a full-blown concept of cultural nationalism was developed. As I discussed, Schiller places the differentiation of both individuals and groups on the same level, regarding both as the result of material determinations. But, as much as Schiller argues for integrating the particulars of the material world with the universality of reason, he nowhere engages the idea of *alternate epistemologies* as it is developed in full-blown cultural nationalism. Schiller does not directly confront the idea that reason itself, instead of being the constant element of humanity, might vary fundamentally from culture to culture. In both a historical and a theoretical sense, this idea of alternate national epistemologies is *unthinkable* to him.

For Schiller, following Kant, reason would not be reason if it were not universal. For Schiller, to give up on the idea of universal reason would be to give up on the idea of human freedom. It would be to turn over to physical causation the complete determination of human identity. Thus Schiller begins with and retains the idea of universal reason, even in those places where he comes closest to positing what we can regard in retrospect as proto-German nationalism. Schiller retains a basic *cosmopolitan* ideal even when working out the concept of the German cultural nation, and this has consequences for the central ambiguous theoretical relationship that critics have noted in the *Aesthetic Letters* between the aesthetic state as a state of mind and the aesthetic state as a political entity.

Given the politically divided entities in which the German-speaking peoples lived during Schiller's time, the only sense that could then be given to the idea of the German nation was of the German cultural nation. Schiller makes his most explicit statement on the concept of the German cultural nation in his prose outline to the poem "German Greatness" (*circa* 1801):

The German Empire and the German nation are two different things. The majesty of the German never rested on the head of his prince. The German has founded his own value apart from politics, and even if the Empire perished, German dignity would remain uncontested. The dignity is a moral greatness. It resides in the culture and in the character of the nation that are both independent of her political vicissitudes . . . While the political Empire has tottered, the spiritual realm has become all the firmer and richer.[12]

Full-blown theories of political nationalism of the mid-nineteenth century contrast the cultural nation and the political nation precisely to highlight the importance of the political nation, and to argue that the cultural nation must culminate in the political nation. In contrast, we see Schiller here making the distinction between the cultural and political nation in order to argue for the importance of the cultural nation distinct from the political nation.

As noted in chapter 1 above, the valuing of the spiritual over the political is a traditional characterization of Romanticism, and is often the basis for criticizing Romanticism for being politically quietist or escapist. Such a criticism is rarely true of any of the major Romantic figures, and such a criticism is certainly not true of Schiller. It is true that the aesthetic "state" in the *Letters* is often identified with a mental state rather than a political entity, and, as can be seen from the quote, Schiller refused to embrace a political German nationalism. But rather than simply adding up as evidence of Schiller's desire to turn away from the political world, these two items actually reveal that Schiller holds a different conception of the political world, one based on universal rationality and the idea that the German cultural nation could be representative of humankind as a whole. For, whatever else it is, the political state that Schiller speaks of as the outcome of the aesthetic education is not the specifically German political nation that becomes the goal of mid-century German nationalism.

Schiller does feel that German culture has a unique role to play, but it is a role in the history of humankind as a whole. For Schiller, the German cultural nation is striving to be representative of universal humanity.[13] The achievements of German culture are conceived along the model of the culture of classical Greece, a cosmopolitan rather than a national legacy. Following Kant's principle, Schiller links the development of all sides of the individual human personality with the development of a collective humanity. For Schiller, these two developments will come together in the developed "state" that is posited as the result of the aesthetic education.

But what precisely does Schiller mean by "state"? In English, the word *state* can apply to both an individual and a group, and from this one can arrive at two different meanings, *state* as the condition of an individual (as in a person's moral state), and *state* as a political collective. As I will show in the discussion of Coleridge in the next chapter, the English word *constitution* has the same central ambiguity. Wilkinson and Willoughby point out that Schiller maintains a distinction in his German terminology between *Stand* (= condition) and *Staat* (= political state).[14] And their precision on this point is an important rebuttal to critics who attempt to criticize Schiller for shifting from one sense of the word *state* to the other to suit his argument. Still, the issue remains that Schiller is clearly trying to argue for an essential connection between *Stand* and *Staat*. The central argument of the *Aesthetic Letters* is, after all, that the aesthetic education will influence the *Stand* of the individual in such a way as to make possible the true political *Staat*. But critics have argued that in the *Aesthetic Letters* we never get to the political state, that instead we remain in the aesthetic state as a condition of mind, and that instead of being a means to a political end, the aesthetic state of mind becomes an end in itself.

A central passage will illustrate why Schiller is open to this kind of criticism. In the twentieth letter, Schiller discusses the process of attaining human freedom. The individual starts under the control of the sensuous drive: "The sensuous drive . . . comes into operation earlier than the rational, because sensation precedes consciousness" (*AL*, xx.2). In order for the individual to attain human freedom, it is necessary that "Reason is to be a power, and a logical or moral necessity to take the place of that physical necessity" (*AL*, xx.3). But, Schiller argues, one cannot simply superimpose the formal drive over the sensuous drive:

> Man cannot pass directly from feeling to thought; he must first take one step backwards, since only through one determination being annulled again can a contrary determination take its place. In order to exchange passivity for autonomy, a passive determination for an active one, man must therefore be momentarily free of all determination whatsoever, and pass through a state [*Zustand*] of pure determinability. *AL*, xx.3

Schiller goes on to identify the aesthetic state as this state of mind free of all determination:

> Our psyche passes, then, from sensation to thought *via* a middle disposition in which sense and reason are both active at the same time. Precisely for this reason, however, they cancel each other out as determining forces, and bring about a negation by means of an opposition. This middle disposition, in which the psyche is subject neither to physical nor to moral constraint, and yet is active in both these ways, pre-eminently deserves to be called a free disposition; and if we are to call the condition of sensuous determination the physical, and the condition of rational determination the logical or moral, then we must call this condition of real and active determinability, the aesthetic. *AL*, xx.4

In this passage we see what appears to be two different accounts of freedom in the aesthetic state. On the one hand, it seems that aesthetic freedom means being free of all determination, that is, being free from both physical and moral restraint. It is this sense of freedom that has led critics to condemn Schiller's aesthetics as being escapist or immoral. It is the interpretation of aesthetic autonomy that we see in the Decadents and in strains of aesthetic modernism.

But if we closely follow the particulars of Schiller's argument here, we can see that he is not arguing for an escape into the aesthetic sphere, and the corollary doctrine of art for art's sake. For the sense of autonomy the subject discovers in the aesthetic sphere comes from feeling the sensuous and the formal drive *reconciled*, not in escaping from both of them. For Schiller, one cannot escape either drive without also ceasing to be human. One must attend to the second part of the sentence: "The psyche is subject neither to physical nor to moral constraint, *and yet is active in both these ways*." The psyche feels free by not feeling subjected to the two drives; it feels itself to actively will both of the drives which now seem harmonious.

This moment of complete equilibrium of the two drives and feeling of human freedom characterizes the ideal aesthetic state of mind. And instead of being a fantasy world into which one permanently escapes, Schiller describes it as an ideal that can never actually be achieved: "Since in actuality no purely aesthetic effect is ever to be met with (for man can never escape his dependence upon conditioning forces), the excellence of a work of art can never consist in anything more than a high approximation of that ideal of aesthetic purity" (*AL*, xx.4). Aesthetic beauty is thus an equilibrium that is not long sustained:

> We have seen how beauty results from the reciprocal action of two opposed drives and from the uniting of two opposed principles. The highest ideal of beauty, is, therefore, to be sought in the most perfect possible union and equilibrium of reality and form. This equilibrium however, remains no more than an Idea, which can never be fully realized in actuality. For in actuality we shall always be left with a preponderance of the one element over the other, and the utmost that experience can achieve will consist of an oscillation between the two principles . . . *AL*, XVI.1

There is the same kind of oscillation between the aesthetic state as an individual state of mind, and the aesthetic state as an actual political entity. Each requires the other, and an advance in one means the advance in the other. One needs a certain level of civilization to get out of the complete grip of physical necessity. But given that prerequisite, the burden then falls on the aesthetic education to develop the individual, which in turn will allow for the further development of the political state.

Critics, however, have long noted Schiller's vagueness about specifying the particular forms of the political state that would bring about this aesthetic education, and the particular forms the political state will assume once it contains a developed citizenry. Indeed, Schiller puts off the practical question until the very end of the work:

> But does such a State of Aesthetic Semblance really exist? And if so, where is it to be found? As a need, it exists in every finely attuned soul; as a realized fact, we are likely to find it, like the pure Church and the pure Republic, only in some few chosen circles, where conduct is governed, not by some soulless imitation of the manners and morals of others, but by the aesthetic nature we have made our own. *AL*, XXVII.12

The short description clearly leaves the practical political details unanswered, but we can read out some important theoretical political consequences. For Schiller here reconnects to a key element of liberalism: the political state can provide the prerequisites for the development of individuals, but the political state on its own cannot achieve that development. Indeed, it is only through the development of the individuals ("by the aesthetic nature we have made our own") that the political state in turn can achieve its most perfect form. The aesthetic state of Schiller is thus fully congruent with the basic liberal enlightenment ideals of individual freedom that Kant had championed. Schiller, like Kant, makes individual freedom the final horizon of his political theory, and he is confident that the freeing up of the individual will inevitably lead to a more perfect political state. It is on this issue that the English figures, Coleridge, Arnold, and Ruskin, have a more vexed relationship, as I will show next.

CHAPTER 4

Symbol, state, and Clerisy: the aesthetic politics of Coleridge

THE PROJECT OF "CHURCH AND STATE"

In chapter 2, I analyzed Coleridge's theo-philosophical account of the symbol in *The Statesman's Manual*. In his last published prose work, *On the Constitution of the Church and State, According to the Idea of Each* (1830), Coleridge presents an account of the English Constitution using the logic of the symbol, and ascribes to the national church (what he calls the Clerisy) the role of the aesthetic sphere. The genesis of *Church and State* was an immediate political issue, the pending bill for the emancipation of Irish Catholics.[1] But Coleridge uses that issue as a jumping-off point to present a systematic culmination of his mature political philosophy, which he had been developing from articles in the periodical *Friend* of 1809 through *The Statesman's Manual* of 1816. *Church and State* presents Coleridge's response to the crises that England was experiencing as the result of industrialization and other aspects of modernization, the forces that Coleridge identifies with the word *progression:* "Roads, canals, machinery, the press, the periodical and daily press, the might of public opinion" (*C&S*, 29).

As his title announces, Coleridge sets out to explain the ideas behind the British state and its national church. Coleridge's argument is that the church and the state had initially been unified according to the originary idea of the constitution, but that the forces of modernization had split these two institutions apart. This split is reflected in the discrepancy between the spirtual and material progress of the nation. The material progress of the nation, its economy, roads, etc., what Coleridge calls "civilization," is proceeding as never before. But the spiritual development of the nation, what he calls "cultivation," is lagging behind, and indeed, suffering from many of the consequences of the nation's material progress.

The last phrase of the title (*According to the Idea of Each*) announces the philosophical idealist method that Coleridge uses in this work. As I discussed in chapter 2, in Coleridge's system of thought, ideas are not just individual mental perceptions but are also forces that guide the development of the intelligible world. The symbols of the Old Testament as Coleridge describes them in *The Statesman's Manual* are clear embodiments of ideas in the material world. However, in describing the relationship between the idea of the English Constitution and its embodiment in actual history, Coleridge acknowledges the greater difficulty in delineating the pure idea because "in the actual realization of every great idea or principle, there will always exist disturbing forces, modifying the product, either from the imperfections of their agents, or from especial circumstances overruling them: or from the defect of the materials" (*C&S*, 37). Coleridge sets out in *Church and State* to reveal the great principles of the constitution that lie behind its occasionally obscure manifestation in actual history

For Coleridge, the English Constitution is thus properly understood as an adaptive system of universal principles that has and will continue to guide the British people through every particular situation that history might present. But as powerful as this political constitution has been and continues to be, the problem it cannot solve is the split of the political nation from that of the national church, the split reflected in the discrepancy between civilization and cultivation. He argues that only a revitalized national church can heal that split. He therefore defends the institution of the national church, but does so in a way that falls outside of the usual terms of the debate about state-established religion.

The argument against the national church by dissenting Protestants was that religion should be a purely private matter, that there should be no connection between church and state, and, consequently, that there should be no national church. In his defense of the general institution of a national church, however, Coleridge does not argue that a national church must be a specific type of Christianity, or even be Christian at all.[2] But he does argue that the national church has an essential function for the well-being of the nation, one that is contained in the original idea of the English Constitution.

Furthermore, Coleridge argues that the original role of the national church was much broader than what is now thought of as religion. He asserts that the national church was originally the central repository of all branches of knowledge and learning, scientific and humanistic. According to Coleridge's account, the narrowing of the conception of the national church occurred because scientific knowledge was split off from it and found its home in commerce and manufacturing, while humanistic knowledge lost its home in the national constitution, and, consequently, its influence on the nation as a whole. Coleridge seeks to rejuvenate the original form of the national church as a broad-based repository of learning, so that it can serve as a unifying force for the state in the face of the fragmenting processes of modernity.

THE ADAPTIVE IDEA OF THE CONSTITUTION AND THE LOGIC OF THE SYMBOL

The line of development to *Church and State* begins with the articles in the periodical *Friend* of 1809, in which Coleridge writes a comprehensive theoretical refutation of the political theorizing of the French *philosophes* ("Metapolitics," as he calls it there) and embraces Edmund Burke's views that government must be based on the traditional practices and institutions of each individual nation.[3] *Church and State* is Coleridge's cumulative attempt to reconcile the cultural nationalism of Burke with the universal rationality of philosophy. He is attempting to express a philosophical and thus *theoretical* account of the traditional ancient constitution, of which Burke was a prominent and often *antitheoretical* defender.

If, however, one takes Burke at his most antitheoretical as the sole representative of political traditionalism, then Coleridge's is an impossible project. For, many of Burke's most famous political arguments are expressed in the course of his attacks on the political theorizing of the instigators and sympathizers of the French Revolution. But what must be remembered is that Burke emerges from a certain political tradition, that of the common law and the ancient constitution, in which reason and tradition were assumed to be in harmony. Faced with political arguments based on "reason" by the proponents of the French Revolution, Burke's strategy was to stress the other pole of the ancient constitution, traditionalism, as an effective counterargument. But Burke's choice of ideological strategy does not preclude other approaches to reconciling the ancient constitution with the challenge of enlightenment reason. Thus, although there is obviously much that is inspired by Burke in *Church and State*, Burke's antitheoretical prescriptivism was not the sole position available to defenders of the ancient constitution, and I will argue that for Coleridge's account of the combined traditionalism and rationality of the constitution in *Church and State*, William Blackstone is a better model.

What makes Coleridge a more complicated traditionalist than Burke is that, although Coleridge equally renounces the antitraditionalism of the French school, he also wants to appropriate the force of their arguments to ground the constitution as a body of rational first principles. Thomas Paine is the most influential advocate of defining political constitutions as sets of first principles, and Coleridge mentions him briefly but significantly early in *Church and State*:

> Ask any of our politicians what is meant by the constitution, and it is ten to one that he will give you a false explanation, *ex. gr.* that it is the body of our laws, or that it is the Bill of Rights; or perhaps, if he have read Tom Payne [*sic*], he may tell you that we have not yet got one; and yet not an hour may have elapsed, since you heard the same individual denouncing, and possibly with good reason, this or that code of laws, the excise and revenue laws, or those for including pheasants, or those for excluding Catholics, as altogether unconstitutional: and such and such acts of parliament as gross outrages on the constitution. *C&S*, 18–19

Paine, Coleridge argues, must be wrong in asserting that the English have no constitution because, as Coleridge points out, everyone routinely appeals to some idea of it. But the problem is not so easily solved. No one in England would deny that there were a set of historical documents and a body of traditional practices generally referred to as the English Constitution.[4] The issue Paine raises is whether in addition to being traditional, the constitution is *rational*, that is to say, whether this set of documents and practices expresses a consistent and equitable set of political principles. Burke could avoid much of the force of Paine's question because Burke appealed to experience and tradition instead of to reason and philosophy in his defense of the English Constitution. But Coleridge cannot disown reason and philosophy. *Church and State* is after all a philosophical account of the English Constitution. It is thus within the context of trying to defend the ancient constitution against the attacks Paine makes on its rationality, charges that Coleridge as an advocate of philosophy has to take seriously, that Coleridge enunciates his aesthetic statism. Coleridge seeks to reconcile the national political traditions embodied in the English Constitution with the universality of reason by positing a symbolic logic for this constitution.

Let us now turn to the specifics of Paine's attack on the English Constitution. The question of the relationship between theory, political principles, and a written constitution had been brought to prominence by Paine's charge in *Rights of Man* (1792) that the English government had no constitution:

A constitution is not a thing in name only, but in fact. It has not an ideal, but a real existence; and wherever it cannot be produced in visible form, there is none... Can then Mr. Burke produce the English Constitution? If he cannot, we may fairly conclude, that though it has been so much talked about, no such thing as a constitution exists, or ever did exist, and consequently that the people have yet a constitution to form.[5]

For Paine, the French Revolution represented an advancement in government in large part because its leaders had brought forth their principles in a written form:

In contemplating the French constitution, we see in it a rational order of things. The principles harmonize with the forms, and both with their origin. It may perhaps be said as an excuse for bad forms, that they are nothing more than forms; but this is a mistake. Forms grow out of principles, and operate to continue the principles they grow from. It is impossible to practise a bad form on anything but a bad principle. It cannot be ingrafted on a good one; and wherever the forms in any government are bad, it is a certain indication that the principles are bad also. *Rights of Man*, 92

As can be seen, Paine begins by asserting that the French constitution is "a rational order of things," and this indicates why an existing, finite, visible, *written* form is required. Because Paine is very much a certain kind of eighteenth-century thinker, he identifies rationality with a set of first principles which are clearly expressed and transparently interpreted.[6] In the political application of reason, such a body of first principles is a written constitution.

When Paine states that "the principles harmonize with the forms," he sets up an important distinction between "principles" and "forms." Of these two terms, let us first consider what Paine means by "forms." Elsewhere, in describing the influence of the American Revolution in making the French Revolution possible, Paine makes an analogy between the forms of the constitution and the forms of language: "The American constitutions were to liberty, what a grammar is to language: they define its parts of speech, and practically construct them into syntax" (*Rights of Man*, 95). Paine's remark that the American constitution is to liberty as grammar is to language makes it clear that the "forms" are first principles *expressed in language*, which, when applied to political ends, yield the structure called the constitution.

In contrast, "principles" on their own, unembodied in language, are intangible, having an "ideal" rather than "real" existence. In making this distinction, Paine is operating with the usual eighteenth-century theory of language, most famously adumbrated by Locke, which distinguishes between ideas in the mind and their expression in the marks and sounds of language. Such a distinction carries with it the danger that the connection between ideas and language, necessary for proper knowing and doing, can be lost. And indeed much of this passage from Paine plays out that anxiety. The importance of the harmony and inseparability of forms and principles is insisted on repeatedly.

For Paine, it is the written constitution that takes on this cementing role: it preserves the principles by binding them to written forms. And, indeed, by the end of the passage, the ambiguity of the word *forms* ("whenever the forms in any government are bad") makes it seem that not only the written constitution is meant, but also all those material manifestations of its enactment (the assembly, the law courts, the army) as well. This seems to guarantee that the written document will overcome any of the possible dangers that might slip in through the gap between the idea and its representation, that is, between political principles and their forms. Thus Paine believes that the only way to ensure that a government is based on good "principles" is to base them on reason and to insure those principles by setting them down in a written form. From the written form of the constitution, the other forms of government, its material institutions, will follow and be safeguarded.

Because Paine considered the traditional political institutions of Europe inequitable and thus irrational, he feared that, without the assurance of a written constitution, any political institution would degenerate into such irrationality. Burke, on the other hand, did not see a necessary crisis between rationality and traditional political institutions and practices. Burke regarded Paine's "rationality" as an abstraction, and believed that "prescription," the gradual adaptation of traditional political institutions over time, ensured that they were adequate and equitable. This is a particularly English form of cultural nationalism. In contrast to the German political situation, Burke can argue that English cultural practices are embodied in its political institutions, since England is a politically united nation.

In these views, as the historian J. G. A. Pocock has shown, Burke was drawing on the tradition of the English common law.[7] In contrast to Paine's rationalist demand for a set of written first principles, the common law operated precisely in those cases where documents containing written first principles no longer existed.[8] The common law is expressed in the form of a set of legal *results*, preserved through the records of past judicial decisions, rather than as a set of *reasons* or *intentions*, as is the case in parliamentary statutes, in the Justinian code, and (as Paine argues) in the new French constitution. But common lawyers such as Blackstone did not on that account consider the common law to lack principles based on reason. They did not make the exclusive appeals to prescription that Burke sometimes makes, that the constitution should be accepted on the force of tradition alone. According to Blackstone, the principles of the common law were there to be brought to light by the interpretive practices of the judge:

a very natural, and very material, question arises: how are these customs or maxims to be known, and by whom is their validity to be determined? The answer is, by the judges in the several courts of justice. They are the depositories of the law; the living oracles, who must decide in all cases of doubt, and who are bound by an oath to decide according to the law of the land.9

But what if the judge should find an aspect of the common law in conflict with reason as he sees it? Should tradition then prevail over reason? In such cases, Blackstone argues, the judge is not overturning the common law but returning it to its original rationality:

even in such cases the subsequent judges do not pretend to make a new law, but to vindicate the old one from misrepresentation. For if it be found that the former decision is manifestly absurd or unjust, it is declared, not that such a sentence was *bad law*, but that it was *not law*; that is, that it is not the established custom of the realm, as has been erroneously determined. *Commentaries*, 51

Thus, far from being a haphazard mass of customs in conflict with reason, the common law according to Blackstone is the very embodiment of reason:

And hence it is that our lawyers are with justice so copious in their encomiums on the reason of the common law; that they tell us, that the law is the perfection of reason, that it always intends to conform thereto, and that what is not reason is not law. Not that the particular reason of every rule in the law can at this distance of time be always precisely assigned; but it is sufficient that there be nothing in the rule flatly contradictory to reason, and then the law will presume it to be well founded. *Commentaries*, 51

We can thus see that Blackstone argues for the implicit rationality of the individual laws of the common law. And Blackstone also argues for the rationality of the overall structure of government that created the laws past and present, the traditional political constitution of England as the King and the two houses of Parliament.

But Coleridge could not simply return to Blackstone's unproblematic confidence that the common law and reason were one and the same. Given the historical situation of Coleridge's time, that was no longer viable. For Blackstone wrote at a time when the possible differences between tradition and reason had not been pushed to a crisis. Moreover, reason as expressed in the common law is for Blackstone a matter for a learned elite, the possession of an interpretative community sharing the same set of beliefs. By the time Burke writes in reaction to the French Revolution, "reason" had become a popular political tool directed against traditionalism. Reason was proclaimed by the supporters of the French Revolution to be universally accessible to the people and the sole determiner of the legitimacy of governments. Thus Paine over-optimistically asserts that "I do not believe that monarchy and aristocracy will continue seven years longer in any of the enlightened countries in Europe. If better reasons can be shown for them than against them, they will stand; if the contrary, they will not" (*Rights of Man*, 156).

Coleridge, however, argues for a means of reconciling reason with experience in a post-revolutionary world and that is through the logic of the symbol. As we saw, Paine identified rationality with a set of first principles that was clearly enunciated and transparently interpreted, and whose meaning was thus finite. But Coleridge's idea of the constitution is based on the symbol. For Coleridge, the constitution is more than a finite set of particular laws; it is a system of universal principles that can be applied to any possible historically particular event. Like a symbol, the constitution is never exhausted by one interpretation. It cannot be, since the common law model of adaptive tradition declares that it is not for an age but for all time. For Coleridge, the written texts traditionally described as composing the constitution (Magna Charta, Bill of Rights, the Settlement Agreement, etc.) express aspects of the idea of the constitution but do not exhaust it in the sense that Paine would have first principles expressed and exhausted in a written constitution.

Coleridge's symbolic model of the constitution is most evident in his description of the "potential power" of the state, in which he argues that the constitution possesses a trans-historical applicability. In chapter 11 of *Church and State*, Coleridge discusses the second of his two "*Conditions* of the health and vigour of a Body Politic" (95). This second condition is that the body politic contain "A due proportion of the *potential* (latent, dormant) to the *actual* Power" (95). Coleridge makes the greatest claims for this balance of powers. He argues that because England has maintained this balance, "for little less than a century and a half Englishmen have collectively, and individually, lived and acted with fewer restraints on their free agency, than the citizens of any known Republic, past or present" (96). Potential power is embodied in the idea of the constitution, which, as Coleridge has argued, is an actual force that guides the history and development of the English nation.

The specific political context of his discussion here is the traditional view that the constitution provides a restraining force against the arbitrary caprices and desires of the King, the Lords, and the Commons. At any historical moment these three do comprise the "actual" power of the nation, but they are restrained from absolute (and thus, for Coleridge, possibly capricious) power by the power of the "self-evolving" idea of the constitution. The lack of this ideal potential power defines for Coleridge the two extremes of government:

A democratic Republic and an absolute Monarchy agree in this; that in both alike, the Nation, or People, delegates its whole power. Nothing is left obscure, nothing suffered to remain in the Idea, unevolved and only acknowledged as an existing, yet indeterminable Right. A Constitution such states can scarcely be said to possess. The whole will of the Body Politic is in act at every moment. *C&S*, 96

The argument of the second sentence recalls the structure of arguments familiar to literary theorists about the opposition between literal (referential) and literary (symbolic) language. This becomes apparent if we substitute *text* for "idea" and *meaning* for "right": "Nothing is left obscure, nothing suffered to remain in the text, unevolved and only acknowledged as an existing, yet indeterminable meaning." These substitutions may seem less gratuitous when we remember that the "idea" that Coleridge is here describing is the English Constitution, which is expressed in (but not exhausted by) a set of actual texts (the Magna Charta, etc.). And insofar as the whole focus of Coleridge's discussion here has been what the "actual" government can or cannot do, and how it is guided and restrained by the "potential" power of the constitution, the questions of meaning and interpretation have obvious ramifications for the determination of what rights do or do not exist.

Those acquainted with Coleridge's writings in other areas will note the similarity between the political and literary arguments here as one of many such analogies in Coleridge's wide-ranging corpus. Thus, John Colmer, the editor of the Bollingen edition of *Church and State*, comments on this sentence:

> In his attitude to language, in his literary criticism, and in his observations on nature and psychological phenomena, as well as in his thoughts on the constitution, C recognizes that there are shadowy areas that defy exact analysis. In such cases to offer exact analysis is to falsify experience. Unfortunately, C's critics have sometimes mistaken respect for obscurity for love of obscurity. *C&S*, 96

Although Colmer rightly points out that this sentence is important for understanding much of Coleridge's thinking, I think that characterizing the issue as one of "obscurity" versus "exact analysis" does not pinpoint what is most important about this analogy between political and literary interpretation. It is not the case that the idea of the constitution is obscure in the usual sense of being forever closed to complete understanding. In the case of the constitution, what is obscure at one time may emerge as a clear force at a later time. Thus Coleridge uses the terms "potential," "latent," and "dormant" to describe it.

It is true that the idea of the constitution is not always perfectly represented in its written forms, and this opens the gap that interpretation must close. But Coleridge's claim to interpretive authority is that he can interpret the constitution more exactly than others (especially those who attend too closely to the obscurities and apparent contradictions of the actual historical documents) precisely because he can perceive the clear idea behind its sometimes imperfect textual manifestations.

Thus it is not the *obscurity* of the constitution, but its *inexhaustibility* that Coleridge praises, its power that is never completely engaged at any historical moment. The inexhaustibility of the English Constitution describes its universal applicability throughout history. Coleridge's claim is that its universal principles have and will continue to guide all particular situations. This claim represents the symbol's reconciliation of universal and particular as applied to the political history of the English nation.

THE CLERISY AND NATIONAL CULTURE

Coleridge's greatest influence on Victorian cultural critics such as Arnold and Ruskin is his concept of the Clerisy, and it remains a point of reference for modern accounts of the goals and value of humanistic learning.[10] The Clerisy is a central element of Coleridge's form of aesthetic statism, and represents an institutional expression of the logic of the symbol. The role of the Clerisy for Coleridge is analogous to the role of the aesthetic education for Schiller. Like Schiller, Coleridge attempts to reconcile the philosophically universal with the historically particular. Coleridge, however, expresses a more explicitly nationalistic narrative of the aesthetic sphere. As I have shown, Schiller describes the fragmentation of the human faculties as the central dilemma of modernity in the *Aesthetic Letters*. Coleridge likewise traces the fragmentation of the human faculties, but he expresses it in terms of a national narrative of the fragmentation of the unity of the original constitution. Like Schiller, Coleridge proposes the aesthetic sphere, in his case in the form of a rejuvenated Clerisy, as a remedy to the fragmentation of modernity.

In chapters 5 and 6 of *Church and State*, Coleridge describes the origin and subsequent breaking up of the original national church, for which he coins the term the "National Clerisy." He describes the original composition of the Clerisy in the following way:

THE CLERISY of the nation, or national church, in its primary acceptance and original intention comprehended the learned of all denominations; the sages and professors of the law and jurisprudence; of medicine and physiology; of music; of military and civil architecture; of the physical sciences; with the mathematical as the common *organ* of the preceding; in short, all the so-called liberal arts and sciences, the possession and application of which constitute the civilization of a country, as well as the Theological. *C&S*, 46

It is important to note that Coleridge does not present his account of the Clerisy as if it were an innovation. He maintains that his description of the national church corresponds to the original idea of the English Constitution. Indeed he justifies his account of the national church by describing the analogous practices of other ancient peoples, the Scandinavian, Celtic, Gothic, and Semitic tribes: "it was, I say, common to all the primitive races, that in taking possession of a new country, and in the division of the land into hereditable estates among the individual warriors or heads of families, a reserve should be made for the nation itself" (*C&S*, 35). Coleridge calls this land and wealth held by the ruling families, "the propriety." That land and wealth set aside for the nation itself, he terms "the nationality."

Coleridge bases his arguments for the Clerisy on the historical basis of the nationality. He makes the distinction between the propriety and the nationality the first great originating act in the establishment of the English state. The propriety, property held in a kind of trust-like relation to the nation, is represented by Parliament. The House of Lords represents the paradigmatic holders of the propriety, namely, the landed aristocracy of the first estate, and the House of Commons represents the holders of the newer forms of moveable wealth (what we now call "private" property), namely, the members of the second estate of merchants, manufacturers, free artisans, and the distributive class.[11]

We can now see that, according to Coleridge's schema, the third estate, the national church, has its own status equal to that of Parliament. Parliament represents the propriety, which is *one half* of the original establishment of the state, but the third estate, the national church, claims the other half, the nationality. The significance of this is that by reference to this original coequal status, Coleridge separates the national church from the governance of Parliament, and gives the Clerisy, his cultural institution, an autonomous and co-equal status next to the traditional political institutions of the state. By this historical narrative, Coleridge lays the basis for his theoretical argument that the Clerisy, a cultural institution, is to be the representative of the *whole nation* rather than Parliament, a political body, which only represents the interests of private property.

According to Coleridge, this original national church of learning (located in a vaguely postulated moment of historical antiquity) subsequently divided into "the practical sciences and the professions" (law and medicine) on the one hand, and, on the other hand, into the national church in the usual exclusively religious sense of the word. Because of this separation, the nonpractical, nontheological aspects of learning, i.e. *the humanities*, lost any institutional home. The overall consequence of this fragmentation of the disciplines of learning was thus the removal of humanistic learning from its proper place, alongside the political institutions of the Crown and Parliament, as a guiding force of the nation. Furthermore, the Clerisy's absence as a guiding force has led to the disparity between *cultivation* (the spiritual progress of the nation) and *civilization* (the material progress of the nation), which for Coleridge is a indication of the crisis of modern society.

The Clerisy is crucial to Coleridge's project of aesthetic statism because it provides a model for joining an immanent account of particular (in this case English) national culture with a transcendent account of universal reason. Coleridge wants the political state to be transcendent in the sense of having a higher authority than that of a mere man-made institution, but he also wants it to be immanent in the sense of having its roots in the history and community of the British people, as expressed in the English Constitution and the Clerisy. Like Schiller, the aesthetic sphere is what connects the two worlds. For Coleridge, the culture embodied in the Clerisy is identified with both the human and the divine, the nationally particular and the universally philosophical. This culture is human; it emerges out of the national spirit and history of the English nation. This culture is also divine; it is eternally true.

Coleridge's aesthetic sphere is, however, to operate through the influence of a guiding cultural elite, the Clerisy, rather than, as in Schiller, the self-willed development of the individual subject.[12] And this points up one of the central problems of *Church and State* when compared to the *Aesthetic Letters*. In *Church and State*, there is no detailed account, as in Schiller, of the way culture develops individual subjectivity. This is because Coleridge often sees individuality as being at the heart of the problem of the dissolution of the organic community. As I have shown, Schiller explicitly draws a central parallel between the autonomy of the aesthetic sphere and autonomy of the individual subject. In contrast, Coleridge downplays the relationship between aesthetic and political autonomy because of his opposition to English liberal individualism, arising out of his critique of English empiricism and political economy.

Although the universality of the culture embodied in the Clerisy is supposed to be what reconciles the individual and the state, in his reaction against English individualism, Coleridge's account of culture often slips into the model of the "common culture" of particular national cultures found in theories of cultural nationalism. In key places, Coleridge argues that culture should be something that *has already constituted the individual*, not something that forms an autonomous individual, as in Schiller. He argues that, in a very real sense, the people do not make up the state; the state makes them. For example, in chapter 7 of *Church and State*, he criticizes the tradition of Lockean empiricism and praises, among others, Sidney, Spenser, and Milton for having properly understood "the IDEA of the STATE," and summarizes such an understanding as "in what sense it may be more truly affirmed that the people (*i.e.* the component particles of the body politic, at any moment existing as such) are in order to the state, than that the state exists for the sake of the people" (*C&S*, 65). Coleridge thus reverses what are the traditional poles of empirical representation.[13] The people of England ("the component particles of the body politic," what would be the primary entities in an empirical model of representation) are not, according to him, represented by the constitution (which would be, in the usual empirical model, the secondary entity, the *re*-presentation). Rather, for him, the constitution is the primary entity which is represented by the secondary entity of the people of England, in the sense that the people and their social and political groups flow from and are guided by the constitutive "Idea" of the constitution. The people are particular enunciations, particular expressions of the whole that is the idea of the constitution.

Coleridge thus ends up emphasizing the priority of the nation rather than, like Schiller, emphasizing individual autonomy. It must be stressed, however, that on a philosophical level, Coleridge never renounces his commitment to the Kantian ideal of the freedom and autonomy of the individual, namely, that political subjects should be seen as ends, never as means. In *The Statesman's Manual*, Coleridge criticizes the impersonality of classical political economy, despite and, indeed, because of its claim to be based on a model of individualist desire. In Coleridge's eyes, classical political economy presents an impersonal model of human agency because it describes the movement of human history as the result of a mathematical averaging of various and opposing individual desires. With this model, there is no way to connect any individual volition directly to the idea of the state, no way for there to obtain the reconciliation between the particular (the individual citizen) and the universal (the political state) promised by the symbol.

But while Coleridge's opposition to empiricism and the classical political economy is undertaken in the name of individual freedom, this opposition leads him to stress the universal rather than the particular pole of the dialectical opposition, and moves him towards positions in practical politics that now strike us as conservative and nationalistic. Thus, in the final analysis, Coleridge is afraid of the freedom of subjectivity to break from the whole. He does not have the faith that Schiller does that the freedom constructed through the aesthetic education will inevitably lead to the freely chosen will to enter into the moral law. Ultimately, Coleridge identifies the subjectivity of political individualism with social fragmentation, that is to say the separation of the individual from the common culture. One can see this theme continue and this separation figured as "anarchy" in the work of Matthew Arnold.

There is a similar paradox in Coleridge's influence on liberal theory. For while Coleridge himself was opposed to the essential principles of individualistic liberalism, his attempts to oppose liberal individualism through an appeal to a sphere of culture became the perfect addition to liberal cultural theory. Culture as described by Coleridge comes to be seen by later liberal theorists like John Stuart Mill as the perfect corrective to the fragmentation of common values that threatened to emerge from the individualist orientation of liberal psychology and *laissez-faire* political economic theory. For, once individualistic liberalism has prevailed in its economic position that commercial relations naturally emerge from the interaction of individuals pursuing their own desires and, consequently, that the freedom to pursue these individual desires should be protected politically, there arises the problem of a shared set of social values. As I discussed in chapter 1, this is a central problem for liberalism's model of the private sphere. If everyone's desires are, at least potentially, unique, how can society maintain a common culture or set of values?

It is because Coleridge attempts to provide both an immanent and transcendent account of culture and society that his arguments for the Clerisy and the importance of cultivation can be taken up even by an avowed individualistic liberal theorist such as Mill. For, Coleridge's philosophy provides a distinct and transcendent sphere of cultural values that yet does not entail a radical critique of traditional property relations or *laissez-faire* economics from the same transcendent stance. His political theory defends traditional property relations on the grounds that they reflect the immanent spirit of the people in their historical development, while preserving the transcendency of the truth claims and cultural values expressed in religion and culture. Thus his philosophy can maintain a transcendent sphere of cultural values while avoiding the radical critique of existing political structures mounted by Paine and the French *philosophes*. Such a model lies behind the paradoxical role granted to high culture after Coleridge, one that, as I will show next, receives its definitive formulation by Arnold: high culture is supposed to be fundamental to the structure of society, but to exist separately from the world of political discourse and action that practically determines that structure.

CHAPTER 5

The best self and the private self: Matthew Arnold on culture and the state

ARNOLD AND COMMON CULTURE

I will make the case for connecting Matthew Arnold with the aesthetic statism of Schiller and Coleridge, but it is important to note that Arnold is often placed in another line, the line of culturally conservative criticism of T. S. Eliot and F. R. Leavis. This is the critical line of descent described by Chris Baldick, in *The Social Mission of English Criticism, 1848–1932*, and Baldick argues that what is central to this line is its rejection of *theory*. Comparing Eliot to Arnold, Baldick writes: "In Eliot's writings there is the same impatience with controversy: his ideal society would change unconsciously without theory or polemic."[1] It is on the issue of being opposed to theory that Baldick distinguishes Arnold from Coleridge: "For the notoriously 'theoretical' Coleridge, practical criticism was a procedure subordinate to critical theory and to philosophy, not antithetical to them. At the very heart of Arnold's major innovations in English criticism is his reversal of Coleridge's position on this point. For him, literary criticism becomes an *alternative* to philosophy, logic, and theory" (232). In many ways, I agree with Baldick's criticisms of Arnold's antitheoretical side, as will be evident in my own criticisms of Arnold's account of the literary touchstones, but Baldick's account ignores the considerable similarities and continuities between Coleridge and Arnold in their projects of aesthetic statism. The issues that Baldick describes as originating in Arnold go back to Romanticism and the opposing political models of cultural nationalism and the liberal state, which I have been tracing in Schiller and Coleridge. For, the larger context of what Baldick describes as an opposition to theory is cultural nationalism, central to which is the concept of common culture, which is the shared set of practices and beliefs that define the national identity. And the larger context of what Baldick denotes by the word *theory* is the separation of the modern subject from the unifying collectivities of the pre-modern world, which, as I discussed in chapter 1, is the central issue behind the crises of modernity.

These alignments are made more explicit by Gerald Graff, who expands on Baldick's argument in his essay on Arnold in the new Yale edition of *Culture and Anarchy*. Graff describes the concept of common culture as a worldview in which there is no gap between experience and reason. This becomes an antitheoretical position because "A really common culture would simply be lived, with no need for its presuppositions, foundations, and beliefs to become an issue for discussion. The word *culture* itself, with its fatal aura of anthropological self-consciousness, betrays the shattering of unself-conscious consensus by divisive modern analysis and theory."[2] Graff concisely sums up the two contrasting meanings given to culture from Romanticism onwards: culture as common culture, the unself-conscious practices of the society; and culture as aesthetic works which promote individual self-consciousness, such as Schiller's aesthetic education. Baldick's argument would place Arnold as a proponent of the first type of culture, and Coleridge as a proponent of the second type. It is significant that the same criticism of embracing the conservatism of common culture that Baldick and Graff make against Arnold can, and often has been, made against Coleridge. My argument, however, is that, like Schiller and Coleridge, Arnold is engaged in a project of aesthetic statism, a project that seeks to reconcile subjectivity and common culture, not to set one up over the other. As I have shown, Schiller seeks this reconciliation in the process of the aesthetic education, and Coleridge seeks it in the symbol and the Clerisy. As I will argue in this chapter, Arnold seeks it in his account of "culture." When Baldick argues that Arnold's account of literary criticism is based on reaffirming the common culture of society, he is correct, but he is only describing half of what Arnold is trying to promote. The other half is individual subjectivity. Thus, while parts of Arnold's writings emphasize the centrality of common culture, in *Culture and Anarchy* Arnold is also committed to preserving a notion of subjectivity in the same Kantian vein as Schiller and Coleridge.

In order to see Arnold's commitment to modern subjectivity, one can compare him to T. S. Eliot. Eliot views modern subjectivity as a symptom of the shattering of a formerly unified culture in which feeling and thought, art and philosophy, individual and group, were united. This idea of lost cultural unity is behind the process that Eliot laments as the "dissociation of sensibility."[3] Baldick describes the critical line from Arnold through Eliot and Leavis as one which views the emergence of modern subjectivity as a kind of historical aberration or tragedy, and which wishes to deny or oppose it in the name of social unity. On the whole, this is accurate for Eliot and Leavis, but only partially true of Arnold. For, as much as parts of Arnold's work foreshadow and make possible this anti-Romantic, antisubjectivistic strain of English cultural criticism, Arnold recognizes modern subjectivity as a necessary historical development, and he seeks to move forward to a political state based on it, rather than seeking to turn back history to a time before it.

Arnold expresses this most clearly in "Democracy" (the introduction to *The Popular Education of France* [1861]), in which he argues that democracy is an inevitable aspect of the change associated with "*the Modern Spirit.*" Arnold argues that the "dignity and authority of the State" ("D," 114) should replace the previous social unifying power of a now fading aristocracy. In *Culture and Anarchy*, Arnold fully develops the relationship between culture and the idea of the state sketched in "Democracy," and it is this work that most fully expresses Arnold's brand of aesthetic statism. But before turning directly to Arnold, one should first consider Arnold in relation to John Stuart Mill. For Mill's *On Liberty* is regarded as spurring Arnold's central arguments against "doing as one likes" in *Culture and Anarchy*.[4]

MILL AND ARNOLD

Criticism has often stressed the general similarities between Arnold and Mill as Victorian culture critics: both argued against the idea that science is the sole means of human development; both argued for the value of poetry and the humanities against rigid forms of utilitarianism.[5] But in relation to the projects of aesthetic statism that I have been tracing, it is important to distinguish Mill and Arnold. Mill is ultimately a *nonaesthetic* liberal theorist, which is to say that, as important as poetry and culture are for Mill in the private sphere, ultimately the aesthetic sphere plays no essential role in his account of the formation of the political state. As indicated in chapter 1 above, Mill espouses a type of liberalism which maintains a strict separation between the public sphere of politics and the state, and the various private spheres of private subjectivity, emotion, and art. Mill maintains a separation between public facts and private desires or values, which the contemporary antiliberal theorist Roberto Unger describes as a central feature of individualistic liberalism: "What distinguishes men from one another is not that they understand the world differently, but that they desire different things even when they share the same understanding of the world."⁶

Unlike Mill, but like Coleridge, Arnold rejects this division between understanding and desire. Unger's description of religious belief as a case in which "the understanding of what we ought to do is part of a comprehension of what the world is really like" (*Knowledge and Politics*, 41) well characterizes the religiously influenced worldview of both Coleridge and Arnold. Although Arnold allows a practical separation between the public and private spheres, he opposes a fundamental separation between facts and values, and indeed it is because he sees them as ultimately connected that he can make the case that culture is a moving force in society.

Because Arnold sees private values and public facts as ultimately connected, he seeks to breach the wall of privacy that Mill sought to erect around subjectivity in *On Liberty*. There, Mill argues that respecting private conscience is the fountainhead of all liberty:

> This, then, is the appropriate region of human liberty. It comprises, first, the inward domain of consciousness; demanding liberty of conscience in the most comprehensive sense; liberty of thought and feeling; absolute freedom of opinion and sentiment on all subjects, practical or speculative, scientific, moral, or theological... Secondly, the principle requires liberty of tastes and pursuits; of framing the plan of our life to suit our own character; *of doing as we like*, subject to such consequences as may follow: without impediment from our fellow-creatures, so long as what we do does not harm them, even though they should think our conduct foolish, perverse or wrong. (my italics)⁷

Although Arnold is clearly sympathetic to Mill's defense of tolerance, he is not willing to make freedom of conscience the center around which all other social issues revolve.⁸ In "Democracy," Arnold criticizes the dissenting religious model of free conscience and the argument that freedom of conscience is the highest good: "It is a very great thing to be able to think as you like; but, after all, an important question remains: *what* you think" (24). The contrast with the central argument of *On Liberty* is clearly evident. Because Mill is so concerned to preserve the first (the ability to think as you like), he mistakenly backs off from the second (the "*what*," the content of those thoughts and desires). But for Arnold it is in the area of content that culture makes itself felt as a social force.

The essential privateness of culture for Mill is reflected in his account of poetry in *Thoughts on Poetry and its Varieties* (1833, 1859) and his account of the state in *Considerations on Representative Government* (1861). Mill's account of poetry is presented by M. H. Abrams in *The Mirror and the Lamp* as the paradigmatic example of expressive aesthetics, the culmination of the Romantic tradition according to Abrams' definition of it. What makes Mill's account Romantic in Abrams' sense is that the essence of poetry is defined as the expression of private subjectivity, the overheard soliloquy. The privateness of the expression distinguishes poetry from rhetoric (what Mill calls "eloquence"):

> Poetry and eloquence are both alike the expression or utterance of feeling. But if we may be excused the antithesis, we should say that eloquence is *heard*, poetry is *over*heard. Eloquence supposes an audience; the peculiarity of poetry appears to us to lie in the poet's utter unconsciousness of a listener. Poetry is feeling, confessing itself to itself in moments of solitude, and embodying itself in symbols, which are the nearest possible representations of the feeling in the exact shape in which it exists in the poet's mind. Eloquence is feeling pouring itself out to other minds, courting their sympathy, or endeavouring to influence their belief, or move them to passion or to action.[9]

Thus, while rhetoric also expresses emotion, it is in the service of swaying an audience and is based on social norms of communication. Poetry is contrasted as a socially disinterested, socially unmediated expression of the individual soul. Mill's use of the term "symbol" here also reflects his private model of poetry. For whereas Coleridge's symbol was given a universal grounding of meaning, Mill's symbols have as their basis the individuality of personal feeling. In contrast to the theological heritage of Coleridge's account of the symbol, Mill's notion of private artistic symbols connects him to the line of modernism of the French *symbolistes*.[10]

We can thus see parallels between Mill's account of poetry and the central argument of *On Liberty* that privacy of conscience must be set aside and protected as a reserve for the individual mind against the ever-encroaching influence of society and its vehicle, the democratic political state. In *Culture and Society*, Raymond Williams nicely sums up the compensatory role culture, and especially poetry, comes to play for Mill, whose strict utilitarian upbringing excluded a place for emotional feeling: "a mind organized in such a way conceives the need for an additional 'department,' a special reserve area in which feeling can be tended and organized. It supposes immediately, that such a department exists in poetry and art, and it considers that recourse to this reserve area is in fact an 'enlargement' of the mind."[11] Culture as a reservoir for feeling thus became a central point of divergence for Mill in his reaction against the strict utilitarianism of Bentham, whose philosophical system was unable to account for the importance of culture. But while Mill's reaction against strict utilitarianism makes a place for high culture, it retains and intensifies the basic liberal split between the public and private spheres. It does so by placing culture, as Williams has pointed out, in a special reserve, separate from the utilitarian principles that determine the public sphere.

The consequences of this separation become most evident in Mill's own account of the state in *Representative Government*. In discussions of *Representative Government*, political scientists have long noted a central tension in Mill's thought. For Mill seeks to have the state be both representative of the society as a whole and be protective of the individual. Sheldon Wolin, for example, questions how Mill can have the state protect the individual from the encroachment of society (the pressure of public opinion), since the very thing that threatens the individual is the fact that the state is increasingly becoming the enforcing agent of the norms of an increasingly uniform society.[12] In other words, as the state becomes more representative of the values and wishes of the majority, such values and wishes will become enforced on the minority.

In order to understand Mill's project in *Representative Government*, it must be remembered that the minority that Mill is trying to preserve is the educated class, which is destined to become a political minority once the inevitable political enfranchisement of the working classes is realized. *Representative Government* proposes several specific political mechanisms to preserve the political influence of the educated minority, such as leaving the drafting of legislation in the hands of experts, and giving multiple votes to the more educated. But the main way Mill proposes to preserve the values of the educated minority is to make the state a vehicle of individual development through which the masses will come to understand and embrace those values.

The state as an instrument of *Bildung* is the model by which Mill proposes to reconcile the two central and opposing political philosophies of liberalism and cultural nationalism. As discussed in chapter 1, Mill contrasts the historicist position that forms of government are unconscious organic developments that emerge from the collective national spirit with the liberal position that governments are rationally created and freely adopted by individuals. Characteristically, Mill seeks a midpoint between the two philosophies and argues that the correct view is that, while there is freedom in choosing forms of government, the degree of this freedom is always fixed within a set of parameters dictated by the history and material conditions of a people.

This idea becomes the basis of Mill's view that government should be a force for education and cultivation: "The first element of good government, therefore, being the virtue and intelligence of the human beings composing the community, the most important point of excellence which any form of government can possess is to promote the virtue and intelligence of the people themselves" (*RG*, 390). Thus, those who are furthest along the line, fully constituted as political subjects, as he sees the educated class in England, should be the ones to design the forms of the government. When the working class participates in these forms they will be developed by that participation towards a state of rational acceptance of them. Thus the working class will be both *formed by* and *formed to* the state. This paternalistic model is Mill's attempt to reconcile the historical and rational formation accounts of government.

Mill's account of the state as the instrument of individual development is similar to Schiller's and, as I will show, Arnold's account of the state.[13] But the crucial difference is that the aesthetic sphere does not occupy the same central place in Mill's account of state formation. And the reason that it does not is because Mill's model of culture and individual development is essentially private. Mill has no way of combining it with the public sphere he lays out in *Representative Government*.

Throughout chapter 3 of *Representative Government*, Mill argues that direct participatory democracy is the ideal form of government, even though it does not necessarily produce superior statecraft. To illustrate this point, he posits the case of "one man of superhuman mental activity managing the entire affairs of a mentally passive people" (*RG*, 400). Now in this case, the government might actually be better run than in a participatory democracy, but such arguments for benevolent despotism "leave out of the idea of good government its principal element, the improvement of the people themselves" (*RG*, 403). While participation in government seems to be Mill's device for effecting the development of its citizens, at the very end of chapter 3, he shifts to representational democracy on the grounds of size, as if nothing else were lost in the transition from direct to representational democracy:

From these accumulated considerations it is evident that the only government which can fully satisfy all the exigencies of the social state is one in which the whole people participate; that any participation, even in the smallest public function, is useful; that the participation should everywhere be as great as the general degree of improvement of the community will allow; and that nothing less can be ultimately desirable than the admission of all to share in the sovereign power of the state. But since all cannot, in a community exceeding a single small town, participate personally in any but some very minor portions of the public business, it follows that the ideal type of a perfect government must be representative. *RG*, 412

But what is also lost is a direct connection between individual development and state formation. As I have shown, such a connection was precisely what Schiller was seeking to provide through his account of the aesthetic sphere in the *Aesthetic Letters*, and it is what Arnold seeks to provide with his account of culture in *Culture and Anarchy*.

One consequence of Mill's private account of culture is that it precludes him from promoting the kind of public cultural institution that Coleridge presents in the Clerisy. Arnold too is against creating an English equivalent of the French *académie*, but for reasons relating to the specific circumstances of English national history. Mill is primarily concerned with the dangers of institutions' encroaching on individual development. Arnold is less concerned with conformity than he is with anarchy, and he describes the virtues of institutions as agents of individual development. He presents an account of culture that is harmonious with, rather than antithetical to, institutions.

CULTURE AND THE STATE

As I discussed in chapter 3, the concept of cultural nationalism is relatively undeveloped in Schiller. In the *Aesthetic Letters*, Schiller seeks to liberate subjectivity from all types of material determinations that might limit its development. Insofar as particular national practices are seen as a limit on such development, his argument opposes them. But for Schiller, local practices had not yet been raised to the status of a worldview, as they are in full-blown cultural nationalism. He shares the general enlightenment view that local practices should and naturally will give way to the cosmopolitan view provided by universal reason. A greater stress on cultural nationalism can be seen in Coleridge's *Church and State*, which reflects English nationalistic feelings resulting from the French Revolution and the war with France. His appeal to the traditions of the English Constitution can be seen as a reaction against the metapolitics of the French. But Coleridge's work still foregrounds the universal elements of the concept of the state and the national church across different nations. With Arnold, however, writing mid-century, the concept of cultural nationalism is full-blown, as can be seen in his essay "Democracy," which is an important precursor to his arguments in *Culture and Anarchy*.

In "Democracy," Arnold proposes a model of the state as the solution to the problems facing England as it moves towards greater democracy. He urges his country to "Look at France! there you have a signal example of the alliance of democracy with a powerful State-action, and see how it works" ("D," 16). But Arnold also asserts that he proposes his emphasis on the state not as a universal model of government, but as appropriate to the specific national characteristics of the English: "one may save one's self from much idle terror at names and shadows if one will be at pains to remember what different conditions the different character of two nations must necessarily impose on the operation of any principle":

If I were a Frenchman I should never be weary of admiring the independent, individual, local habits of action in England, of directing attention to the evils occasioned in France by the excessive action of the State; for I should be very sure that, say what I might, the part of the State would never be too small in France, nor that of the individual too large. Being an Englishman, I see nothing but good in freely recognising the coherence, rationality, and efficaciousness which characterize the strong State-action of France, of acknowledging the want of method, reason, and result which attend the feeble State-action of England; because I am very sure that, strengthen in England the action of the State as one may, it will always find itself sufficiently controlled. "D," 16–17

This is Arnold's general approach to cultural nationalism, acknowledging its basis and then seeking improvement through an infusion of elements outside of itself. Arnold takes the same approach to the different identity blocks within England itself, the divisions of class. Thus, in "Democracy," he argues for the benefits of state influence on middle class schools, because "by giving to schools for these classes a public character, it can bring the instruction in them under a criticism which the stock of knowledge and judgement in our middle classes is not of itself at present able to supply" (22). This is precisely the role of culture as Arnold fully develops it in *Culture and Anarchy*, to challenge the stock notions of class-determined perspectives.

In *Culture and Anarchy*, Arnold's project of aesthetic statism presents culture in terms we now associate with arguments for avant-garde art, namely, that it shakes up custom and dispels stock perceptions. Reminiscent of Schiller, Arnold speaks of the Hellenistic outlook, the perspective identified with culture, as promoting "an unimpeded play of thought" and giving "our consciousness free play and enlarging its range"(*C&A*, 88, 100).[14] However, throughout the work, Arnold seems to present two seemingly contrasting meanings to the word *culture*. On the one hand, he identifies culture with Hellenism, as that which promotes individual and social perfection by shaking off stock perceptions. Culture is initially defined in the preface as "being a pursuit of our total perfection by means of getting to know, on all the matters which most concern us, the best which has been thought and said in the world, and, through this knowledge, turning a stream of fresh and free thought upon our stock notions and habits, which we now follow staunchly but mechanically" (*C&A*, 5). On the other hand, he attributes the origin of culture to *establishments* such as the national church, and the universities: "The great works by which, not only in literature and art, and science generally, but in religion itself, the human spirit has manifested its approaches to totality, and a full harmonious perfection, and by which it stimulates and helps forward the world's general perfection, come, not from Nonconformists, but from men who either belong to Establishments or have been trained in them" (*C&A*, 10–11). But how can Arnold reconcile the progressive powers attributed to culture with the seemingly conservative orientation of the establishments? The establishments would seem to represent those very traditional and stock perceptions that he is seeking to challenge.

It is in his attempt to reconcile these two accounts of culture – culture as promoting new subjectivity and culture as embodied in the national establishments – that Arnold is engaged in a project of aesthetic statism. The way he seeks to reconcile these two accounts of culture is to argue that the culture embodied in the national establishments provides a perspective that is more encompassing than the limited stock perceptions of any of the subgroups of the nation. For Arnold, the establishments embody a truly *collective* national culture. He argues that the breadth of this collective national culture is the quality that can counteract what he sees as the narrow individualism of the English religious dissenting tradition, which he calls the "Hebraism" of the English middle class. By its breadth, Arnold argues, the culture embodied in the establishments will cultivate "new sides and sympathies": "establishments tend to give us a sense of a historical life of the human spirit, outside and beyond our own fancies and feelings" (*C&A*, 15).

Arnold's opposition to the dissenting tradition's model of individualist subjectivity and his appeal to the collective culture of the establishments are thus both parts of the goal of "being in contact with the main stream of human life" (*C&A*, 23).[15] And the connection between these two positions is especially evident in chapter 2 of *Culture and Anarchy*, where Arnold gives his account of the proper concept of the state. The state is presented in terms of this project of widening and correcting the partial perspective characteristic of British individualism. The chapter title, "Doing as One Likes," expresses Arnold's view of the essence of this individualism: "the central idea of English life and politics is *the assertion of personal liberty*" (*C&A*, 50). Arnold argues that, historically, this tradition of political individualism emerged as a reaction against the inequalities of the feudal system of privileges. He then poses the question: What happens now that feudal privileges have been swept aside? "As feudalism, which with its ideas and habits of subordination was for many centuries silently behind the British Constitution, dies out, and we are left with nothing but our system of checks, and our notion of its being the great right and happiness of an Englishman to do as far as possible what he likes, we are in danger of drifting towards anarchy" (*C&A*, 50).

The solution Arnold offers to the danger of anarchy comes from outside of the British individualist tradition: it is the concept of the state. "We have not the notion, so familiar on the Continent and to antiquity, of *the State*, – the nation, in its collective and corporate character, entrusted with stringent powers for the general advantage, and controlling individual wills in the name of an interest wider than that of individuals" (*C&A*, 50–1). But if the state represents something other than individual citizens, what does it represent? Arnold works his way towards an answer to this question by first arguing against those who would try to identify the state with the interests of either the aristocratic, middle, or working classes (the Barbarians, Philistines, and Populace, as they are dubbed in chapter 3).

Arnold argues that basing one's identity on class interest prevents one from understanding what the state should be. The class-identified self, which Arnold describes as "our everyday selves," can only understand government as something that protects individuals and their rights by keeping other individuals at bay. But such a model of government can offer no solution when the problem at hand is the very fragmentation of society itself: "By our everyday selves, however, we are separate, personal, at war; we are only safe from one another's tyranny when no one has any power; and this safety in its turn, cannot save us from anarchy. And when, therefore, anarchy presents itself as a danger to us, we know not where to turn" (*C&A*, 64). The place to turn, Arnold answers, is culture. Culture, which Arnold's critics had criticized as powerless to influence the political problems of the day, emerges, by its very nonpartisan nature, as the only possible solution to the problem. Culture,

Arnold argues, is the only thing that can bring out the "best self" within the citizen, the classless self which can then actualize the idea of the collective state:

> But by our *best self* we are united, impersonal, at harmony. We are in no peril from giving authority to this because it is the truest friend we all of us have; and when anarchy is a danger to us, to this authority we may turn with sure trust. Well, and this is the very self which culture, or the study of perfection, seeks to develop in us; at the expense of our old untransformed self... our poor culture, which is flouted as so unpractical, leads us to the very ideas capable of meeting the great want of our present embarrassed times! We want an authority, and we find nothing but jealous classes, checks and a deadlock; culture suggests the idea of *the State*. We find no basis for a firm State-power in our ordinary selves; culture suggests one to us in our *best self*. *C&A*, 64–5

Arnold's "best self" is thus described in opposition to one's public identity, the class-based "everyday" self. For a reader coming from the perspective of British individualism, the opposite of the public self is the private self, the individual personal identity we maintain in the shelter of our homes, the private self of *On Liberty*. But Arnold reverses these associations of the terms "public" and "private." He argues that the best self is "impersonal." It is in our everyday public identity that we are "separate, *personal*, at war."

Instead of the paradigm of British individualism, Arnold is using the paradigm seen in Kant and Schiller, which identifies the essence of human freedom (the best self) with a subjectivity that is unconstrained by material determinations. As in Schiller's account of the aesthetic state of mind (*Stand*), from the perspective of Arnold's best self, facts and values will cease to be in conflict. It is on the basis of freeing the best self-identity from material determinations that Arnold can make the case that the interests discovered by such a best self are in the best interests of the community as a whole (the state), rather than individual or partisan interests. In this sense, he argues that culture promotes a "total" perspective. And he contrasts the total perspective of culture with what he sees as the partial and thus necessarily limited perspectives of historically and materially formed interests.

Arnold thus opposes individualistic liberalism because, for him, such "individualism" is really always conditioned by class. Thus when I am most in touch with culture, for Arnold, I am least an individual in the individualistic liberal sense of desiring my materially *class-bound* preferences. Arnold's culture thus cuts itself off from the actual existing cultures of the society and from the material conditions that produce those cultural practices. For him, culture allows individuals to liberate themselves from their class-bound perspectives. This act of liberation could be regarded as itself an individualistic gesture, but Arnold argues that in doing so these individuals are actually entering a new kind of disinterested class, the "aliens" or "remnant" in Arnold's terms. For Arnold, culture allows one to be an individual in the sense that it allows one to escape the conformity of one's class, but ultimately he sees a unity arising from all the individuals thus freed. The idea of the remnant thus displays the same notion of self-willed membership in a community separable from material conditions that we saw Schiller describing as the aesthetic state in the conclusion of the *Aesthetic Letters*. Culture therefore promotes a kind of individuation which is compatible with entering a truly unified community, which is what Arnold identifies as the true meaning of the idea of the state.

Thus through culture, each individual will independently come to the recognition of right reason, and, on this basis, individual cultivation will have the effect of promoting the perfection of society as a whole, i.e. the state. Like Kant and Schiller, Arnold stresses that the two processes are everywhere intertwined:

> the expansion of our humanity, to suit the idea of perfection which culture forms, must be a *general* expansion. Perfection, as culture conceives it, is not possible while the individual remains isolated; the individual is obliged, under pain of being stunted and enfeebled in his own development if he disobeys, to carry others along with him in his march towards perfection. *C&A*, 33

Thus there is the need of the state, through its establishments, to promote the kind of culture which will lead to the cultivation that will ultimately perfect the state itself. It is on this side of the argument for promoting the culture of the establishments that Arnold seems to fall into the conservatism of the "common culture" paradigm that Baldick and Graff criticize, the idea that the subjectivity of the individual should be fully congruent with the traditional collective culture of the society. However, what distinguishes his account of culture in *Culture and Anarchy* from a reactionary appeal to the common culture of the cultural nation is that Arnold's "culture" is only *proleptically* common culture. In the same way that the "minority" that Mill sought to preserve in *On Liberty* and *Representative Government* was an educated one, so too the culture that Arnold exalts is, at the time he writes, minority culture, in the sense that only an educated minority of people possess it, namely, "the aliens." Arnold believes that what he calls culture is destined to become "common" because it is universal, based on right reason, but it remains at his historical moment, minority culture.

THE TOUCHSTONES: TRADITION AND CULTURE

Granted Arnold's premises, his attempt to present a progressive model of establishment culture is theoretically coherent. Where he opens himself to charges of bad-faith cultural conservatism is not in *Culture and Anarchy* itself, but in the literary absolutism of the account of the literary touchstones in "The Study of Poetry" (1880). The same issue is at stake, namely, how to reconcile the progressive claims made for poetry with the idea of an established literary tradition. But the reason Arnold is unable to reconcile these two element successfully here is that he refuses to make an inclusive theoretical case for the aesthetic sphere, like Schiller, or to make a theoretical case for traditionalism, like Coleridge. Arnold presupposes the justifications he should be arguing for, and, as a consequence, appears to express an arbitrary valuation of tradition for its own sake.

What is at stake in Arnold's untheoretical account of the touchstones is not the basic issue of the conflict between aesthetic universality and cultural relativism. Like Kant, Schiller, and Coleridge, Arnold opposes cultural relativism and avowedly believes in something called "right reason" that transcends nationality and class. But, as we saw in Schiller's account of the aesthetic education, a universalistic account of truth and aesthetic experience does not necessarily entail cultural traditionalism. As I argued, Schiller's claims for the aesthetic education are based on the universality of the aesthetic experience, not a particular cultural canon, let alone a traditional one. For Schiller, tradition *per se* plays no role in determining aesthetic adequacy.

One might argue that Arnold's famous definition of culture in *Culture and Anarchy* as "the best which has been thought and said in the world" (*C&A*, 5), by its "has been," already limits culture to what has been approved by tradition. But as I have argued, the overall argument of *Culture and Anarchy* stresses culture as an ongoing process, and none of the arguments there preclude an open and developing cultural canon. New aspirants to the canon of culture would certainly be tested against traditional culture, but the standard by which they would be judged will be explicit, namely, their adequacy to develop the total human perspective. Arnold seems to abandon this potentially inclusive model of the canon in "The Study of Poetry." In *Culture and Anarchy*, he identifies culture with breadth, change, and development. In "The Study of Poetry," he seems to identify culture with specific traditional works for seemingly no other reason than that these have been approved by literary tradition.

Arnold's changed identification of culture is especially apparent if one compares the defense of the establishments in *Culture and Anarchy* with the defense of the touchstones in "The Study of Poetry." In *Culture and Anarchy*, the establishments are praised for the same reason that the concept of the state is, that is, for promoting social unity. In the case of the established church, Arnold opposes what he sees as the social fragmentation caused by the Dissenters' insistence on finding their own forms of worship to suit their individual consciences. Arnold argues that the forms of worship of the Church of England are *good enough* to serve, and that fixed forms of worship free one up to concentrate on other aspects of one's life and overall development:

One may say that to be reared a member of an Establishment is in itself a lesson of religious moderation, and a help towards culture and harmonious perfection. Instead of battling for his own private forms for expressing the inexpressible and defining the undefinable, a man takes those which have commended themselves most to the religious life of his nation; and while he may be sure that within those forms the religious side of his own nature may find its satisfaction, he has leisure and composure to satisfy other sides of his nature as well. *C&A*, 11

Arnold might have made the analogous argument about the literary canon and, like Schiller, have argued that for poetry, like any manifestation of culture, the absolute uniqueness of each work is less important than the general adequacy of the aesthetic sphere to develop the individual. But even in the passage above, Arnold's tendency to assume an unargued adequacy for traditional forms can be seen. His tendency is to put the burden of proof on those who want to reject traditional forms. This tendency is evident at the conclusion of *Culture and Anarchy* in Arnold's famous antiradical arguments for preserving the current political structure as a prerequisite to developing a better one: "for us . . . the framework of society . . . is sacred; and whoever administers it, and however we may seek to remove them from the tenure of administration, yet, while they administer, we steadily and with undivided heart support them in repressing anarchy and disorder; because without order there can be no society, and without society there can be no human perfection" (135).

In "The Study of Poetry," Arnold goes further in the identification of tradition and culture, and regards the literary touchstones as *embodiments* of right reason, rather than as representative examples of culture:

> Indeed there can be no more useful help for discovering what poetry belongs to the class of the truly excellent, and can therefore do us most good, than to have always in one's mind lines and expressions of the great masters, and to apply them as a touchstone to other poetry. Of course we are not to require this other poetry to resemble them; it may be very dissimilar. But if we have any tact we shall find them, when we have lodged them well in our minds, an infallible touchstone for detecting the presence or absence of high poetic quality, and also the degree of this quality, in all other poetry which we may place beside them. "SP," 168

Throughout the essay, Arnold takes a specific approach, preferring "to have recourse to concrete examples" over "abstract" definitions of poetry ("SP," 170). But his appeal to "tact" here goes beyond what might be defended as a healthy empiricism. For, the appeal to tact implies a special sensibility that makes entry into the aesthetic sphere seem an exclusionary rather than a universal process. And this passage further presents a problematical account of the relationship between form and content in the touchstones. For the paradox of Arnold's account of the touchstones is that, on the one hand, he argues that they are useful because they are specific forms, but, on the other hand, he argues that form alone does not determine great poetry. Arnold insists on the inseparability of substance and style in poetry: "The superior character of truth and seriousness, in the matter and substance of the best poetry, is inseparable from the superiority of diction and movement marking its style and manner" ("SP," 171). But if this is true, what then, as many critics have pointed out, is the point of presenting very brief touchstones with minimal context, as Arnold does in the essay?

The way to understand these paradoxes of the touchstones is to recognize that Arnold is tacitly relying on the claims of the Coleridgean symbol, even though he has formally renounced the theology that provided the theoretical basis for Coleridge's claims for the symbol. This is illustrated by Arnold's famous opening of "The Study of Poetry," in which he proclaims that poetry will supercede religion as the main cultural influence on society. The ascension of poetry over religion represents the last stage of that strand of Higher Biblical Criticism that sought to defend the continuing relevance of the Bible by reinterpreting it in metaphorical terms. As I have shown, in *The Statesman's Manual* Coleridge engages in metaphorical reinterpretations of the Bible, but he insists that such metaphors are really philosophical truths grounded by the reconciliation of universal and particular in the symbol. As in the case of the adaptive English Constitution, it is the universality of the Bible that allows for constant new interpretations of its literal text.

But Arnold is not prepared to mount this sort of philosophical defense for the truth of biblical metaphor. And thus, as he argues in the opening of "The Study of Poetry," if what is important is metaphor, then poetry can deliver it much more immediately and powerfully to the masses of the modern age than can the Bible, whose metaphoricity had become obscured because its religious defenders had sought to defend its claims to literal truth:

There is not a creed which is not shaken, not an accredited dogma which is not shown to be questionable, not a received tradition which does not threaten to dissolve. Our religion has materialised itself in the fact, and now the fact is failing it. But for poetry the idea is everything; the rest is a world of illusion, of divine illusion. Poetry attaches its emotion to the idea; the idea *is* the fact. "SP,"161

But despite the purely metaphorical truth value that Arnold claims for poetry in the opening of "The Study of Poetry," his claims for the touchstones tacitly rely on the special theo-philosophical claims made by Coleridge for the truth of the symbol. For, according to Arnold, the touchstones are supposed to be uniquely particular and yet universal; they are supposed to be part of a temporal tradition and yet provide a timeless standard of judgment. Arnold's account of the touchstones thus reveals the contradictions of a completely secularized and non-philosophical account of Coleridge's symbol. Mill, as we saw, assimilates literary symbols to the private subjectivity of the artist. But, for Arnold, literary symbols, like any manifestation of culture proper, must ultimately carry a universal social meaning. If poetry expresses particular human emotions, these must nonetheless serve as expressions of universal human nature.

Arnold's account of the touchstones thus brings to the forefront the fundamental tensions in his account of culture. In *Culture and Anarchy*, Arnold wants to establish culture as a force in its own right. He does not want to reduce culture to any particular religious doctrine or the views of any particular class of society. But in his attempts to maintain the autonomy of culture, he runs the risk of undermining any possible foundation for the purported universal truth value of culture. Since Arnold refuses to define culture in terms of any particular theological position, he cannot claim the divine universal truth of Coleridge's account of the symbol. And since Arnold refuses to identify culture with the practices and attitudes of any actually existing groups or classes of people, he cannot claim a sociological ground of truth. As Raymond Williams points out, for Arnold, "Culture was a process, but he could not find the material of that process, either, with any confidence, in the society of his own day, or, fully, in a recognition of an order that transcends human society" (*Culture and Society*, 127).[16] The other possible basis for the truth value of culture would be the philosophical basis of the aesthetic sphere that Schiller seeks to provide in the *Aesthetic Letters*. But Arnold's rejection of "abstract" theory in "The Study of Poetry" precludes him from turning in that direction. The consequence of Arnold's impasse has been that odd combination of features that so often characterizes English literary criticism: the highest possible claims made for the individual and social benefits of literature, combined with a lack of any detailed theoretical account of how and why literature provides such benefits. In this critical atmosphere, for which Arnold himself is partially responsible, Arnold's own project of aesthetic statism has remained obscured.

CHAPTER 6

Aesthetic kingship and queenship: Ruskin on the state and the home

As a theorist of aesthetic statism, John Ruskin seems both very close to and very far from our twentieth-century worldview. In his sociological analyses of art in *The Stones of Venice* and his critiques of classical political economy in *Unto this Last*, Ruskin seems very contemporary, but in his embrace of medieval ideals of chivalry and domesticity he seems hopelessly retrograde. This is particularly a problem with *Sesame and Lilies*. One could try to solve the problem by writing off *Sesame and Lilies* as a flawed production of Ruskin's failing latter years. But Ruskin produced this work in the same decade as *Unto this Last*, and he himself argues that it emerges out of the same social vision as his critiques of political economy. For example, in his preface to the 1882 edition of *Sesame and Lilies*, he concludes by stating that "it was written while my energies were still unbroken and my temper unfretted; and that, if read in connection with *Unto this Last*, it contains the chief truths I have endeavoured through all my past life to display" (*WR*, XVIII, 52). Clearly, *Sesame and Lilies* held a high place for Ruskin as an expression of his mature thought. In line with his own estimation, I will argue that, however flawed it might now seem to us, this work indeed expresses Ruskin's final attempt to express the value and role of the aesthetic sphere as a guiding force for society, something that he had been striving to do throughout his long career of writing on aesthetic and social issues. In this final account, the aesthetic sphere is gendered. Kingship, the masculine side, is represented by a canon of great books that are personified as leaders. Queenship, the feminine side, is represented by domestic woman, who is aestheticized as a symbol of moral goodness.

For Ruskin, we can broadly define the course of the relationship between the aesthetic sphere and state formation, in both its individual and political senses, in the following way. In his early work, especially evident in *Modern Painters*, volume II (1846), Ruskin expresses a religiously based account of beauty in both nature and art as a system of divine "types" (symbols) expressing God's moral ordering of the universe. In the course of losing his religious belief, he moves towards what we would now call a sociological account of art. This turn in his thought is most famously expressed in "The Nature of Gothic," chapter 7 of the second volume of *The Stones of Venice* (1853). Through his analysis of architecture, which he sees as the most socially representative art, Ruskin argues that art expresses and reflects the fundamental conditions and values of the society that produces it. Art becomes a barometer of the state of the society as a whole. While Ruskin never gives up on art as a positive force in society, he can no longer claim that art is the main guiding one. The problem as expressed in *The Two Paths* (1859) is that historically, the perfection of art seems to go hand in hand with the moral disintegration of societies. Ruskin's argument at this point is that art reflects rather than causes this disintegration, but the problem remains that art *per se* cannot prevent such a decline. Because Ruskin comes to see that good art is the result of a good society, he turns his attention to the general conditions that lead to the good or ill of society, its wealth and "illth," as he calls it. His critiques of classical political economy, most famously expressed in *Unto this Last* (1860), reflect this aspect of his thinking. But in a final turn in his thought, Ruskin returns to the idea of the aesthetic sphere as the main guiding force of society. He expresses this in *Sesame and Lilies* (1865) through the ideas of kingship and queenship, which correspond to great books and women as the respective repositories of eternal truth and goodness.

BEAUTY, TYPES, AND MORAL MEANING

The most comprehensive account of Ruskin's early aesthetic thought is found in the second volume of *Modern Painters*. One of Ruskin's main goals here is to argue against the idea that the value of beauty lies in the gratification of the senses. Indeed, he rejects the very term *aesthetic* because of its root in the Greek word *aísthēsis*, meaning perception or sensation, which he regards as too closely associated with the senses. Drawing on the Platonic and Aristotelian idea of *theōría*, which is the contemplation of the moral good, Ruskin describes what he calls the Theoretic faculty, which "is concerned with the moral perception and appreciation of ideas of beauty" (*WR*, IV, 35).

In *Modern Painters*, vol. II, Ruskin presents a particularly Christian-based account of the moral ideas revealed by beauty. For him, these ideas are based on the presupposition of the divinely ordained nature of the universe. This is particularly evident in the chapters on "typical" beauty. Ruskin derives this term from the religious doctrine of types.[1] Without entering into the details of the specific sectarian traditions that inform Ruskin's conception of types, we can note the overall connection to the theological background that we have discussed in connection with Coleridge's account of the symbol.[2] In his notes to the 1883 edition, Ruskin explains the term "typical" as meaning "any character in material things by which they convey an idea of immaterial ones" (*WR*, IV, 77). The chapter titles convey the specifically religious symbolism that Ruskin reads out of the forms of beauty: "Of Infinity, or the Type of Divine Incomprehensibility"; "Of Unity, or the Type of the Divine Comprehensiveness"; "Of Repose, or the Type of Divine Permanence," etc.

The second broad category of beauty that Ruskin describes is what he calls "vital beauty." Whereas Ruskin's account of typical beauty was based on relatively broad formal categories that could appear in the forms of either animate or inanimate objects, vital beauty specifically concerns living creatures, both the animal kingdom and humankind. Like his analysis of typical beauty, Ruskin sees vital beauty as symbolic of the moral virtues: "There is not any organic creature but, in its history and habits, will exemplify or illustrate to us some moral excellence of deficiency, or some point of God's providential government, which it is necessary for us to know" (*WR*, IV, 156). Thus he speaks of "the foulness of the sloth, and the subtlety of the adder, and the rage of the hyaena" (*WR*, IV, 156), working his way up to more morally exemplary creatures such as the industrious ant and bee.

This moral scale continues with the vital beauty of human beings. But although one might expect humanity as a species to be at a higher level of perfection than any species of animal, Ruskin argues that a complete spectrum exists with humanity itself: "No longer among the individuals of the race is there equality or likeness, a distributed fairness and fixed type visible in each; but evil diversity, and terrible stamp of various degradation" (*WR*, IV, 176). In analyzing the upper end of this spectrum, Ruskin describes how "the conception of the bodily ideal" is reached for human beings, both in an appearance of healthy vigour and, more importantly, in those aspects of appearance that reflect the virtues of intellect and moral feelings. As I will show, Ruskin's idea of the beauty of moral feeling will return as a central idea in his analysis of domestic woman in *Sesame and Lilies*.

Taking an overview of Ruskin's account of the symbolism of beauty in the second volume of *Modern Painters*, one can note similarities but also some important differences from Coleridge's account of the symbol. Like Coleridge's symbols, Ruskin's "types" express the universal through the particular. In what initially seems a similarity to Coleridge, Ruskin emphasizes that the particular form of the type is as important as the universal truth it represents. But there is an important difference of emphasis between Coleridge and Ruskin on the particularity of the symbol. For, in stressing the particularity of the type, Ruskin is focusing on its particularity in the sense of what its material form looks like. The subject of *Modern Painters* is after all about beauty and appearance. Of course, as I have shown, for Ruskin appearance is never skin-deep; it also carries a moral meaning. Nonetheless, it is at the level of appearance that Ruskin stresses particularity, not at the level of autonomous subjectivity, which is Coleridge's focus on the particularity of the symbol.

Indeed, the question of subjective autonomy is particularly problematic for Ruskin in his early work. As I have shown, Coleridge's account of the symbol is an attempt to reconstruct traditional religious symbolism according to the paradigms of contemporary philosophy, specifically the philosophy of modern subjectivity. Now, it is true that in volume II of *Modern Painters*, Ruskin does engage contemporary aesthetic philosophy, particularly Burke. But overall it is clear that in his early aesthetic theory, Ruskin is not so much reconstructing religious typology according to the terms of modern philosophy as he is simply asserting the traditional worldview of evangelical Christianity in the face of it. As Landow points out in *Aesthetic and Critical Theories of John Ruskin*, the central tension in Ruskin's aesthetic theory in the second volume of *Modern Painters* is reconciling the objective account of divine types with the subjective element of aesthetic response. And once Ruskin begins to lose the religious belief that underpins the objectivity of divine types, the question of the subjectivity of aesthetic response presents itself as a major problem in his attempt to assert the central moral basis of the contemplation of beauty and art. For Ruskin, the concept of society eventually comes to take over the role of the encompassing system that gives moral meaning to art.

AESTHETIC LABOR AND SOCIETY

Chapter six of the second volume of *The Stones of Venice*, entitled "The Nature of Gothic," has been seen by both Ruskin and his commentators as a major turning point in his conception of the relationship between art and society. Ruskin begins by arguing that in order to understand the material forms of any style of architecture, one has to understand the "Mental Power or Expression" behind the style: "What characters, we have to discover, did the Gothic builders love, or instinctively express in their work, as distinguished from all other builders?" (*WR*, x, 183). Ruskin describes six "moral elements of Gothic," Savageness, Changefulness, Naturalism, Grotesqueness, Rigidity, and Redundance, the details of which I will not enter into here. All these elements are ultimately connected to what Ruskin sees as the essential Christian element in the nature of Gothic, which is that Christianity recognizes the value of every soul, even and especially flawed souls.

Ruskin argues that, outside of a few great artists, no human worker can achieve a dual perfection in expression and finish. And the more ambitious the undertaking, the more difficult it is to reach perfection: "For the finer the nature, the more flaws it will show through the clearness of it; and it is a law of this universe, that the best things shall be seldomest seen in their best form" (*WR*, x, 190). In the case of architectural decoration, the consequence of this truth defines two basic approaches. Since one cannot practically achieve both ambitious forms and perfected finish, one can either choose to have simple forms well-finished, or have ambitious forms with flaws. The first approach turns the workman into a kind of machine by dictating a set of simple forms that are to be produced to a certain standard of finish by the strict following of procedures. This approach, in its various permutations, is seen in the "servile ornament" of the ancient Greeks and Egyptians, as well as in modern ornament (what Ruskin calls "Revolutionary ornament") "in which no executive inferiority is admitted at all" (*WR*, x, 188–9).

The second basic approach is embodied in the Gothic. The spirit of the Gothic does not hide its flaws, because flaws are the marks of free human beings: "in the medieval, or especially Christian, system of ornament, this slavery is done away with altogether; Christianity having recognized, in small things as well as great, the individual value of every soul" (*WR*, x, 189–90). Gothic decoration thus allows a reflection of the human soul of each workman in its particular humanity, reflecting both the good and the imperfect.

To use Marxist terms (which this strain of Ruskin's thought would eventually merge with in the work of William Morris), Ruskin is contrasting alienated and engaged labor. Ruskin argues that it is alienated labor that fuels the class conflicts of his time: "It is verily this degradation of the operative into a machine, which, more than any other evil of the times, is leading the mass of the nations everywhere into vain, incoherent, destructive struggling for a freedom of which they cannot explain the nature to themselves" (*WR*, x, 194). For Ruskin here, as in *The Two Paths* and *Sesame and Lilies*, the democratic elements associated with the emergence of modern individual subjectivity are destructive aberrations from the naturally hierarchical nature of the universe. For him, the discord of modern individualism emerges out of the alienated slavery of modern work, and he looks back on the past where "in all ages and all countries, reverence has been paid and sacrifice made by men to each other, not only without complaint, but rejoicingly; and famine, and peril, and sword, and all evil, and all shame have been borne willingly in the causes of masters and kings" (*WR*, x, 195).

By comparing Ruskin's account in "The Nature of Gothic" to the previous accounts of aesthetic statism, one can see that Ruskin's ideal of the inventive craftsman embodies the Schillerian ideal of the aesthetic state on the level of individual *Bildung*. The engaged connection between the workman and his work that Ruskin describes is analogous to the reconciliation between subjective spirit and material world in the individual that Schiller describes as the achievement of the aesthetic state in the *Aesthetic Letters*. But there are significant differences between their conceptions of the aesthetic state. The first difference is that Ruskin's individual aesthetic state is achieved in engaged practice, rather than in a state of autonomous detachment as described in Schiller's account. Ruskin's individual aesthetic state is centrally focused on the world of work, the world of political economy, and the material connections between them. Through this emphasis, Ruskin removes the aesthetic sphere from the autonomous character I have shown in various degrees in the previous theorists of aesthetic statism. (However, as I will show in my analysis of *Sesame and Lilies*, the domestic sphere ultimately comes to take the place for Ruskin previously occupied by an autonomous aesthetic sphere.)

A second major difference is that Ruskin describes a very different relationship between individual aesthetic development and political development. As I have shown, the ideal moment of reconciled aesthetic labor becomes a model against which Ruskin criticizes the alienated labor of modern society. Given this model of the ideal state for both the worker and society at large, the problem then becomes how to achieve it in modern society. In addressing this problem, Ruskin ultimately moves in the opposite direction from the theories of aesthetic statism that I have previously examined. For Schiller, Coleridge, and Arnold, art is ultimately both the primary model and the primary guide to both individual and society. As we saw, especially as formulated by Schiller, art serves as both the model and medium of reconciliation for the subject. It is through immersion in the aesthetic sphere that the subject can achieve a reconciliation between the subjective and objective aspects of his or her experience. And subjectivity thus reconciled and freed by art becomes the force that will reconstruct the political state.

Now as in Schiller, art for Ruskin is both a model for and a medium of individual and social development. But Ruskin arrives at the conclusion that art alone is not enough to effect the transformation of society. Ruskin comes to see art as part of a social whole, of which it is both a determiner and a reflection. This is a position that he develops in detail in *The Two Paths*, particularly in the first lecture "The Deteriorative Power of Conventional Art over Nations," and in another lecture he writes around the same time as *Sesame and Lilies*, "The Relation of National Ethics to National Arts" (1867).

Using the peoples of the Indian subcontinent and Highlands of Scotland as initial examples, in "The Deteriorative Power of Conventional Art over Nations," Ruskin explores the relationship between achievement in art and national morality. In terms of art, Ruskin finds India "a race rejoicing in art, and eminently and universally endowed with the gift of it," while in the case of the Highlands "you have a people careless of art, and apparently incapable of it" (*WR*, XVI, 262). But in terms of national morality, the judgment is the reversed: "Out of the peat cottage come faith, courage, self-sacrifice, purity, and piety . . . out of the ivory palace come treachery, cruelty, cowardice, idolatry, bestiality" (*WR*, XVI, 263).

Ruskin argues that this pattern is not an isolated case, but part of an apparently universal pattern: "if we pass from the Indian peninsula into other countries of the globe; and from our own recent experience, to the records of history, we shall still find one great fact fronting us, in stern universality namely, the apparent connection of great success in art with subsequent national degeneration" (*WR*, XVI, 263). This pattern represents, of course, a major problem for Ruskin, who had since *Modern Painters* stressed the moral value of art. Ruskin's argument in the defense of art is that art does not cause this "national degeneration," but rather reflects the general state of moral degeneration that advanced civilizations often come to have.

But how is this degeneration revealed in a nation's art? Ruskin argues that although "the art of India is delicate and refined, it has one curious character distinguishing it from all other art of equal merit in design – *it never represents a natural fact*" (*WR*, xvi, 265, original emphasis). This kind of art "indicates that the people who practice it are cut off from all possible sources of healthy knowledge or natural delight" (*WR*, xvi, 265–6). For Ruskin the cause of degeneration in societies is the people's turning away from nature and focusing on the pursuit of their own subjective interests and pleasures. In the practice of art this becomes "art, followed as such, and for its own sake, irrespective of the interpretation of nature by it," which "is destructive of whatever is best and noblest in humanity" (*WR*, xvi, 268).

Now, as we saw in "The Nature of Gothic," the achievement of the aesthetic state for the craftsman is a synthesis of the subjective powers of the worker with the objective materials he works with and the forms of nature he adopts for his design. But this synthesis is lost when the art of a nation turns away from nature and turns inward to contemplate only its own forms: "a time has always hitherto come, in which, having thus reached a singular perfection, she [Art] begins to contemplate that perfection, and to imitate it, and deduce rules and forms from it; and thus to forget her duty and ministry as the interpreter and discoverer of Truth" (*WR*, xvi, 269). What Ruskin is describing is subjectivity lingering on itself, and I will have more to say about Ruskin's antipathies towards the self-determining nature of modern subjectivity. But let me focus for now on one of the central consequences of Ruskin's account of the relationship between art and the degeneration of the moral character of nations. Ruskin's analysis seeks to exonerate art of the charge of causing the degeneration of national morality. For, as he argues, art is a reflection, not a cause. But, if Ruskin's account of art as social reflection indicates that art does not cause the degeneration, then it also indicates that art on its own cannot halt that degeneration.

Thus Ruskin's sociological account of art removes art from the guiding role we have seen in the previous aesthetic statists. For Ruskin, there is no point in attempting to improve national art in the hopes of improving the overall state of the nation, because, as he puts it in the "The Relation of National Ethics to National Arts" lecture:

We cannot teach art as an abstract skill or power. It is the result of a certain ethical state in the nation, and at full period of the national growth that efflorescence of its ethical state will infallibly be produced: be it bad or good, we can no more teach nor shape it than we can streak our orchard blossom with strange colours or infuse into its fruit a juice it has not drawn out of the sap. *WR*, XIX, 166

Thus, although Ruskin is engaging in sociological observations about art, he does not embrace a position of cultural relativism regarding great art. Ruskin continues to hold that great art is great, whether or not a particular nation can appreciate or achieve that greatness. What he is questioning is the idea that merely exposing people to the great art of the past will improve the present sensibility of the nation. For Ruskin, the existence of great art is evidence of the ethical superiority of the societies of the past that made such art possible. But Ruskin questions whether it does the citizens of the present any good to contemplate this art, if all such art can do is stand as evidence of a reconciliation of subject and object that they can never achieve under the conditions of modern society. The issue for Ruskin becomes how to achieve the good society in which working conditions will allow everyone to experience some version of aesthetic reconciliation in the form of satisfying engaged labor. This view forms the basis of Ruskin's movement from questions of art to questions of the working conditions that make art possible, his movement to a sustained critique of political economy and its alienated modes of production that are the focus of *Unto this Last* and his other economic writings.

KINGS' TREASURIES

As I have shown, Ruskin wants the reconciliation provided by good art but comes to see that, in order to achieve good art in modern society, it is first necessary to improve the irreconciled medium of existing society. Thus, in order to sustain art, Ruskin has to go outside of art, to political economy, in order to create the material conditions that will make good art possible. Now, I began this chapter with Ruskin's comments in the preface to the 1882 edition of *Sesame and Lilies* in which he connects this work to *Unto this Last* as comprising "the chief truths" he had sought to express throughout his life. In *Sesame and Lilies*, Ruskin describes guides for transforming society. But, instead of expressing this through the language of political economy, he uses the language of high culture and domesticity. In *Sesame and Lilies*, Ruskin presents an account of culture that takes on the guiding role for society that his sociological account of art had seemed to undermine. In his previous work, Ruskin's analysis of art had broadened out into an analysis of the material and sociological factors that determine the creation of works of art. From this perspective, art became a reflection rather than a guide to society. In *Sesame and Lilies*, Ruskin asserts a sphere of truth and goodness that exists independently of the materially determined world. Because it is independent of the forces that determine existing society, it can be a guide to society. This sphere is embodied in the eternal truths expressed by great books and the sustaining goodness of domestic woman. These are Ruskin's ideal rulers of society, its true kings and queens.

The first lecture is entitled "Sesame: of Kings' Treasuries." At the end of the lecture, Ruskin reveals the pun of the title, which evokes the Arabian Nights story of the magic word *sesame* that opens the doors to a treasury. But what Ruskin seeks to describe in his lecture is not gold, but "the treasures hidden in books" (*WR*, xviii, 54). He begins by arguing that, although education is mostly regarded in his time as a means for worldly advancement, education should be seen as a good in itself. And he further argues that great books are written in the same spirit, not for selfish motivations but as a result of the need to say something which the writer "perceives to be true and useful, or helpfully beautiful": "whatever bit of a wise man's work is honestly and benevolently done, that bit is his book or his piece of art. It is mixed always with evil fragments – ill-done, redundant, affected work. But if you read rightly, you will discover the true bits, and those *are* the book." (*WR*, xviii, 61; original emphasis). Ruskin's ideas here can be compared with Arnold's account of true culture as classless and selfless. As shown previously, for Arnold the process of coming to the truth involves renouncing one's limited actual class perspective and cultivating one's best self, which is impersonal and universal. Ruskin likewise argues that the true process of reading entails "putting ourselves always in the author's place, annihilating our own personality, and seeking to enter into his" (*WR*, xviii, 75). If readers faithfully attempt this process, they will find that their own opinions are "a matter of no serious importance," and indeed Ruskin avers that "unless you are a very singular person, you cannot be said to have any 'thoughts' at all" (*WR*, xviii, 76). Ruskin sums up by stating:

> You will not be able, I tell you again, for many and many a day, to come at the real purposes and teaching of these great men; but a very little honest study of them will enable you to perceive that what you took for your own "judgment" was mere chance prejudice, and drifted, helpless, entangled weed of castaway thought . . . that the first thing you have to do for them, and yourself, is eagerly and scornfully to set fire to *this*; burn all the jungle into wholesome ash-heaps, and then plough and sow. *WR*, xviii, 78

What Ruskin is describing in his account of the process of learning from great books is the act of submitting to one's betters, who should naturally be one's leaders. This idea of submitting to one's leaders is the central way that Ruskin unfolds his metaphor of books as kings. And kingship is central to Ruskin's hierarchical conception of society. This is a point he foregrounds in distinguishing his social program from that of socialism in *Unto this Last*:

> if there be one point insisted on throughout my works more frequently than another, that one point is the impossibility of Equality. My continual aim has been to show the eternal superiority of some men to others, sometimes even of one man to all others; and to show also the advisability of appointing such persons or person to guide, to lead, or on occasion even to compel and subdue, their inferiors according to their own better knowledge and wiser will. *WR*, XVII, 74

This model of compelling and subduing is apparent throughout *Sesame and Lilies*. In defending the "old-fashioned" values of the work in the preface to the 1882 edition, Ruskin asserts that "the second lecture, in its very title, 'Of Queens' Gardens,' takes for granted the persistency of Queenship, and therefore of Kingship, and therefore of Courtliness or Courtesy, and therefore of Uncourtliness or Rusticity. It assumes, with the ideas of higher and lower rank, those of serene authority and happy submission" (*WR*, XVIII, 51).

But despite the language of domination and submission, Ruskin argues that this kingship of books is, unlike actual earthly kings, based on a moral and intellectual merit. And it is according to this framework of great books as elite leaders that Ruskin inscribes a traditional literary canon within his idea of a guiding aesthetic sphere. As I have shown, in his account of the guiding role of the aesthetic, Schiller had stressed the reconciling quality of the aesthetic *per se*, which, as I argued, did not depend on or entail prescribing a specific canon of aesthetic works. Also, Arnold's account of culture in *Culture and Anarchy* was not theoretically dependent on a narrow traditionalist canon (although this is an element that Arnold later introduces through his account of the literary touchstones). Ruskin's canon in "Of Kings' Treasuries," although never explicitly specified, seems both narrow and traditional. For example, Ruskin uses a passage from Milton's *Lycidas* to illustrate the process of proper reading, but asserts that "this writer, from whom I have been reading to you, is not among the first or wisest," and that "with the greater men, you cannot fathom their meaning; they do not even wholly measure it themselves, – it is so wide. Suppose I had asked you, for instance, to seek for Shakespeare's opinion, instead of Milton's, on this matter of Church authority? – or for Dante's?" (*WR*, XVIII, 77). A canon that relegates Milton to the second rank is demanding indeed. But we can see in this passage that for Ruskin writers of the first order like Shakespeare and Dante become more than writers expressing individual ideas. Writers of this first order create meanings that they cannot fully comprehend themselves. Like Coleridge's symbolic English Constitution, they are inexhaustible transcendental sources of meaning.

According to Ruskin, the great writers express themselves in strong words but "in a hidden way and in parables in order that he may be sure you want it" (*WR*, XVIII, 63). That they do so is a bit of a puzzle for Ruskin: "I cannot quite see the reason of this, nor analyse the cruel reticence in the breast of wise men which makes them always hide their deeper thought" (*WR*, XVIII, 63). One of the reasons that this is a puzzle for Ruskin is that he generally correlates great art with a perfection of expression. In his analysis of the grotesque, for example, he describes it as the work of those who strive to represent beauty but whose level of intellectual perception and technical skill is inadequate to the task.[3] Since great writers could express themselves perfectly clearly and choose to express themselves emblematically, Ruskin sees a moral reason behind it: "They do not give it you by way of help, but of reward; and they will make themselves sure that you deserve it before they allow you to reach it" (*WR*, XVIII, 63–4). Ruskin turns to the analogy of gold, which reconnects to his central metaphor of books as treasuries. Like gold, the meaning of great books is hidden and requires mining and smelting: "Do not hope to get at any good author's meaning without those tools and that fire; often you will need sharpest finest chiselling, and patientest fusing, before you can gather one grain of the metal" (*WR*, XVIII, 64).

QUEENS' GARDENS

Towards the end of "Of Kings' Treasuries," Ruskin states that one comes to great books "not merely to know from them what is True, but chiefly to feel with them what is just" (*WR*, XVIII, 80). It is this quality of feeling with, of sympathy, that connects kingship to Ruskin's ideal of queenship as he expresses it in the second lecture, "Lilies: Of Queens' Gardens." For sympathy is what "the pure woman has above all creatures; fineness and fullness of sensation, beyond reason; – the guide and sanctifier of reason itself. Reason can but determine what is true: – it is the God-given passion of humanity which alone can recognise what God has made good" (*WR*, XVIII, 80). In stressing sympathy as the central role of woman, Ruskin expresses one of the central ideas associated with Victorian domestic ideology.[4] According to this ideology, the role of woman was to provide moral guidance to man through sympathy and the maintenance of a domestic haven from the public world. Sarah Stickney Ellis' well-known domestic manual *The Women of England* (1839) expresses this idea of the separation between the spheres and duties of men and women, with men furthering their "worldly aggrandizement" in the public sphere, and women "guarding the fireside comforts of his distant home . . . clothed in moral beauty."[5] Victorian domestic ideology has its most famous literary expression in Coventry Patmore's poems on the theme of "the angel in the house," and indeed Ruskin approvingly quotes lines from Patmore in the course of the "Queens' Gardens" lecture. Ruskin reflects many of the commonplace ideas of Victorian domestic ideology, but expresses them through the context of the relationship between culture and the state.

In "Of Queens' Gardens," Ruskin turns to the idea of the state and the different roles of the sexes in relation to it. He first considers the connection between the concepts of kingship and the state:

> There is, then, I repeat – and as I want to leave this idea with you, I begin with it, and shall end with it – only one pure kind of kingship; an inevitable and eternal kind, crowned or not; the kingship, namely, which consists in a stronger moral state, and a truer thoughtful state, than that of others; enabling you, therefore, to guide, or to raise them. Observe that word "State"; we have got into a loose way of using it. It means literally the standing and stability of a thing; and you have the full force of it in the derived word "statue" – "the immovable thing." A king's majesty or "state," then, and the right of his kingdom to be called a state, depends on the movelessness of both: – without tremor, without quiver of balance; established and enthroned upon a foundation of eternal law which nothing can alter, nor overthrow. *WR*, XVIII, 110

Like Arnold, Ruskin connects the right to lead with one's place in the ladder of moral cultivation: kingship is correlated with "a stronger moral state, and a truer thoughtful state." And like Arnold, the word *state* for Ruskin denotes both an advanced mental state of cultivation in individuals and the political entity instituted and guided by the individuals who possess such advanced cultivation.[6]

Ruskin proceeds to distinguish by gender the processes of cultivation that lead to the state. Since he has identified great books with the kingly power, the question arises of the role of the queenly power: "what special position or kind of this royal authority, arising out of noble education, may rightly be possessed by women?" (*WR*, XVIII, 110). Ruskin argues that the role of women in the process of cultivation leading to the perfection of the state is in maintaining the domestic sphere, the "Queens' Gardens" of the title of the lecture. He seeks to illustrate the role of women in maintaining the stability of the state by a review of exemplary women in literature. He asserts that "Shakespeare has no heroes; he has only heroines," (*WR*, XVIII, 112) and reviews the heroines of the plays. He then considers the heroines in the Scottish novels of Sir Walter Scott, before finally revealing his guiding model in the depictions of "knightly honour and love" (*WR*, XVIII, 116) in Dante and the courtly love poets. Adopting this model of knightly chivalry, Ruskin calls for the "spiritual submission" (*WR*, XVIII, 117) of men to women, asserting that "in all Christian ages which have been remarkable for their purity or progress, there has been absolute yielding of obedient devotion, by the lover, to his mistress" (*WR*, XVIII, 119).

Ruskin's initial assertions of the authority of woman are prolonged and emphatic: "I say *obedient*; – not merely enthusiastic and worshipping in imagination, but entirely subject, receiving from the beloved woman, however young, not only encouragement, the praise and reward of all toil, but, so far as any choice is open, or any question difficult of decision, the *direction* of all toil" (*WR*, XVIII, 119). But it eventually becomes clear that Ruskin is not proposing that women actually govern the state. For, Ruskin draws a distinction between "determining" and "guiding" functions. The former is associated with man, whose power is "active, progressive, defensive." Man is "eminently the doer, the creator, the discover, the defender" (*WR*, XVIII, 121). But woman's power "is not for rule, not for battle, – and her intellect is not for invention, or creation, but for sweet ordering, arrangement, and decision" (*WR*, XVIII, 122). For Ruskin, women do not guide by what they *do*. (Indeed it is hard to see what they could do, given the way Ruskin exclusively attributes all active functions to men.) Rather, they guide by what they *are*, and what they *feel* for others.[7]

As in other Victorian domestic ideology, for Ruskin the importance of the female domestic sphere is that it serves as a shelter from the hardening effects of the male public sphere:

This is the true nature of home – it is the place of Peace; the shelter, not only from all injury, but from all terror, doubt, and division. Insofar as it is not this, it is not home; so far as the anxieties of the outer life penetrate into it, and the inconsistently minded, unknown, unloved, or hostile society of the outer world is allowed by either husband or wife to cross the threshold, it ceases to be a home; it is then only a part of that outer world which you have roofed over, and lighted fire in. *WR*, XVIII, 122

For Ruskin, the role of the woman in this private sphere is to serve others: "She must be enduringly, incorruptibly good; instinctively, infallibly wise – wise, not for self-development, but for self-renunciation" (*WR*, XVIII, 123). But whereas in typical Victorian domestic ideology, the essence of this sympathetic role lies in its circumscribed application to the private family sphere, Ruskin expands its application to his concept of the state. Thus, far from being private, the sympathy of women becomes a public function, even a public duty:

There is no suffering, no injustice, no misery, in the earth, but the guilt of it lies with you [women]. Men can bear the sight of it, but you should not be able to bear it. Men may tread it down without sympathy in their own struggle; but men are feeble in sympathy, and contracted in hope; it is you only who can feel the depths of pain, and conceive the way of its healing. *WR*, XVIII, 140

For Ruskin, the social function of women has always been, and should always remain, sympathy, and this emerges in this last quotation in the anger behind his belief that they are now neglecting that role in the modern era. Ruskin goes so far in insisting on the connection between domesticity and the good of the state that he collapses one of the basis tenets of domestic ideology, namely that there is a strict separation between the public world of men and the domestic world of women:

Generally, we are under an impression that a man's duties are public, and a woman's private. But this is not altogether so. A man has a personal work or duty, relating to his own home, and a public work or duty, which is the expansion of the other, relating to the state. So a woman has a personal work or duty, relating to her own home, and a public work or duty, which is the expansion of that. *WR*, XVIII, 136

Ruskin's opposition to a strict division between the public and private spheres here is consistent with his overall rejection of the tenets of individualistic liberalism that animate his criticism of classical political economy.

In the end, women, or, rather the chivalric idealization of woman, comes to take over the higher good previously contained for him in religion and art, which Ruskin had linked together in his early accounts of beauty. A connection can thus be seen between Ruskin's early account of vital beauty in *Modern Painters*, vol. II, and the representation of domestic woman in *Sesame and Lilies*. In the former, Ruskin described vital beauty both in terms of the functional beauty of a creature well-formed to fulfill some purpose and the vital beauty of moral goodness. In the latter, the vital beauty of domestic woman is expressed in terms of moral perfection rather than in activity. Women fulfill their function by being, rather than doing, which is attributed to men. Because their "function" is nonpurposive, they come to resemble art objects. They become like Kant's account of the work of art, purposive without a purpose.[8]

Ruskin's aestheticization of domestic woman thus removes autonomy from the female subject. It is the paradoxical role of his ideal woman to be a guide to all society and yet be unable to guide herself. It is precisely this sort of paradox of Victorian domestic ideology that Elizabeth Barrett Browning challenges in *Aurora Leigh* when she has her heroine ask:

> am I proved too weak
> To stand alone, yet strong enough to bear
> Such leaners on my shoulder? poor to think,
> Yet rich enough to sympathise with thought?[9]

SUBJECTIVITY, GENDER, AND SOCIETY

Although Ruskin is in many ways the most engaged in the questions of practical social reform of all the previous aesthetic statists, when viewed against the narrative of modernity and modern subjectivity, he is often the most antimodern. In terms of the roles of women, Ruskin is obviously, and even by his own admission in the preface to the 1882 edition, against the modern tide of change.[10] But viewing the question of women's domestic roles from a broader historical perspective, there is an interesting way in which the ideology of domesticity, which Ruskin upholds, can itself be seen as the result of the same modernizing processes of capitalism that Ruskin elsewhere opposes. For domestic ideology as a whole can be seen as part of a central aspect of modernization, the division of labor, specifically, the division of labor according to gender roles. Ruskin is blind to this because of his essentially non-historical analysis of women. As I have shown, he develops a very sophisticated understanding of the influence of historical and sociological factors on determining the role and condition of the male workman. But his account of women is based on literary depictions of chivalry from which all historical context has been removed.

Interestingly enough, traces of the historical context of Victorian domesticity can be glimpsed in that other famous example of Victorian domestic ideology, Ellis' *Women of England*. Ellis' work is commonly viewed as celebrating the splendor of woman confined within the domestic haven of the home. But if one reads more than the often-quoted passages, one can see that for her, the separation of work and home, instead of being the ideal state of affairs, is rather a very problematic historical development that threatens her basic concept that middle-class virtue is based on work.[11] Ellis' well-known claims for a separate domestic sphere as a haven for morality against the corrupting influences of the world of political economy can thus be seen as a compensatory response to the historical moment, rather than, as in Ruskin, a celebration of the timeless role of woman. For Ellis, the separate domestic sphere is a way of limiting the dangers she perceives as resulting from the already existing separation between home and workplace, a separation which threatens her conception that the virtue of the state is sustained by the labor of the middle class.

Ellis' domestic ideology can be understood as her attempt to make the best of what she sees as an already existing bad situation – the separation of the sites of men's and women's work under the effects of modernization and industrialism. And thus while we expect and do indeed find Ellis to be opposed to women working outside of the home, we should also note that she is likewise displeased with the fact that *men* are now increasingly working outside the home. Their place of work is no longer the family shop, which represents for her that pre-industrial space in which men's and women's work was not so sharply divided. In *The Women of England*, the few glimpses we get of men in their workplaces are bleak, and emphasize their isolation from all the comforts of domesticity. Ellis highlights the separation of work and home that produces what she sees as the twin problem of the age – overworked men and overly idle women.

Overall, Ellis is critical of large-scale capitalism because its effect has been to concentrate labor in workplaces outside of the home, resulting in the decline of the home-based family shop, and the dichotomizing of the public and private spheres. The model of the state for her is not the *laissez-faire* public sphere of classical political economy, but rather the unity of public and private symbolized in the home of the first household itself – that of Queen Victoria. It is this unity that Ellis emphasizes in dedicating *The Wives of England* (1843) to the Queen: "let us never forget, that in the person of our beloved QUEEN we have the character of a wife and a mother so blended together with that of a sovereign, that the present above all others ought to form an era in British history, wherein woman shall have proved herself not unworthy of the importance attached to her influence, and her name."[12]

Historians of women's labor confirm Ellis' sense that the movement of work out of the home was the fundamental factor in the emergence of modern domesticity roles. Bridget Hill, drawing in part on the earlier work of Ivy Pinchbeck, traces the shift in the eighteenth century from the household economy, in which "the work of the vast majority of women (as well as men) in the eighteenth century" took place, to the modern model of the separation of the home and work site: "What happened to that economic and demographic unit, at whatever time, profoundly affected the work opportunities of women, the nature of women's work, and the conditions under which it was performed."[13] In their comparison of women's labor in England and France, *Women, Work, and Family*, Louise A. Tilly and Joan W. Scott come to a similar conclusion.[14] Ruskin himself was well-versed in the historical development of the capitalism he so trenchantly criticized, but he did not seem to realize the relationship between the development of capitalism and the separate spheres doctrine of gender roles. Ironically, Ruskin ends up upholding the gender division of labor produced by the forces of capitalism that he so opposed on other fronts.

But it is not just to women that Ruskin would deny the autonomy of modern subjectivity. He is wary of modern subjectivity and becomes especially critical of its manifestations in political economy and modern democracy. He criticizes modern subjectivity as a historical development, even though he embraces many of the traditions that lead to it. For example, in "The Nature of Gothic," Ruskin argues that Christianity recognizes the individual value of every human soul, and he praises the building practices of the Gothic style because they allow a reflection of the individual soul of each workman in all his individual human imperfection. In these ways, he praises the spirit of Protestant individualism that Hegel, for example, traced as one of the fountainheads of modern subjectivity. And indeed he describes the "indirect causes holding a far more important place in the Gothic heart, though less immediate in their influence on design" as "strength of will, independence of character, resoluteness of purpose, impatience of undue control, and that general tendency to set the individual reason against authority, and the individual deed against destiny, which, in the Northern tribes, has opposed itself throughout all ages, to the languid submission, in the Southern, of thought to tradition, and purpose to fatality" (*WR*, x, 241–2). But Ruskin goes on to caution against the "error in excess" in both the northern and southern spirits. And, like Arnold's criticisms of the English Puritan legacy of "doing as one likes," Ruskin warns that the Gothic spirit "may go too far in its rigidity, and like the great Puritan spirit in its extreme, lose itself either in frivolity of division, or perversity of purpose" (*WR*, x, 242).

Coleridge also has similar reservations about many aspects of modern subjectivity, and his reticence comes from many of the same religious sources as Ruskin. But Coleridge was also the follower of Kant and a poetic celebrator of subjectivity, and both these facts come through in his stress on the autonomy of the symbol. One can particularly contrast Ruskin with Coleridge on this point. Ruskin does make glancing remarks on the real human nature of biblical agents in his discussion of the Gothic. Ruskin asserts that the Bible, like Gothic decoration, records the human imperfection of the subjects it depicts: with "a great indifference" it "sets down, with unmoved and unexcusing resoluteness, the virtues and errors of all men of whom it speaks, often leaving the reader to form his own estimate of them, without an indication of the judgment of the historian" (*WR*, x, 235). But Ruskin's emphasis here is on the nonjudgmental style of the depiction of biblical agents, not on the autonomous subjectivity of these individuals, as in Coleridge's account of the symbol. As I have shown, by drawing analogies between the proper subordination of elements in a work of art and in society, Ruskin's ideal society retains the hierarchical features of medieval society.[15] This aestheticization of hierarchy finds its final form in the gendered aesthetic sphere of kingship and queenship in *Sesame and Lilies*.

CHAPTER 7

The aesthetic and political spheres in contemporary theory: Adorno and Habermas

In this final chapter, I will examine the legacy of aesthetic statism in twentieth-century theory. I began chapter 1 by citing Raymond Williams' analysis of how, during the course of the nineteenth century, an opposition developed in literary theory between subjective experience and social and political institutions. I would argue that the majority of twentieth-century aesthetic theories continue this opposition. Most twentieth-century aesthetic and literary theories continue to be based on the idea that aesthetic works constitute a special category. But, instead of connecting the special status of the aesthetic sphere to social and political formation, as was the case in aesthetic statism, most twentieth-century theory defines the special nature of aesthetic works in ways that separate the aesthetic sphere from the public sphere.

In the broadest theoretical terms, one can describe the major aesthetic theories of the twentieth century as falling towards one or the other of the two poles of objectivity and subjectivity that aesthetic statism attempted to unify. On the objective side, one can locate the various formalist approaches that focus on the interplay of formal elements within the artwork. On the subjective side, one can locate aesthetic theories which describe both the origin and effect of art in terms of private subjective experience. In general, both of these approaches minimize, ignore, or exclude the connection between the aesthetic sphere and political formation.

Theories of objective formalism are descendants of the tradition of "art for art's sake," a concept originating in Pater which reaches its most advanced expression in twentieth-century aesthetics, particularly in certain strains of aesthetic modernism.[1] Such theories regard the question of an artwork's effect on the individual viewer, or on society as a whole, as aesthetically irrelevant. (This, as I have argued, is the view that Woodmansee mistakenly ascribes to Schiller.) Because such formalist aesthetic theories exclude the dimension of audience response, they obviously exclude any concern with the public sphere. But just because an aesthetic theory concerns itself with audience response does not mean that it will also concern itself with the public sphere. The other major group of twentieth-century aesthetic theories, those based on individual subjectivity, do precisely emphasize the effect of art on the viewer, but do so in a way that neglects the role of the aesthetic in social and political formation. The paradigmatic example of this kind of aesthetic theory is John Stuart Mill's account of poetry, which, as we saw, locates the value of poetry in individual private experience. Like aesthetic statism, Mill's aesthetic theory places the work of art in a special category and makes art valuable to the development of the individual subject. But unlike aesthetic statism, in which the development of the individual through aesthetic education is intrinsically linked with the development of the political state, Mill's aesthetic education is described exclusively in terms of individual private searches for meaning. As I have shown in chapter 1, Mill's account of poetry has largely been the model through which the legacy of Romanticism has been viewed in the twentieth century.

The majority of twentieth-century aesthetic theories are some variant of these formalist or private subjectivity approaches. One of the few approaches that has sought to continue the tradition of aesthetic statism by positing an intrinsic connection between the aesthetic and political spheres has been the work of those theorists associated with the Frankfurt school. In this chapter, I will focus on two of the most prominent theorists of this school, Theodor Adorno and Jürgen Habermas. Individually, each is an influential theorist who carries on the tradition of aesthetic statism by analyzing the aesthetic sphere in relation to the political crisis of modernity. And analyzing their aesthetic theories together reveals the great dilemma that the aesthetic sphere faces in the twentieth century: either retain its autonomy and renounce its claims to transformative social influence, or renounce its autonomy and be absorbed into the broader sphere of social practices as a whole.

Adorno occupies the first alternative by maintaining the unique autonomy of the aesthetic work, and his defense of aesthetic autonomy comes at the cost of attenuating the connection between aesthetic works and social and political practices. On the other side, the logic of Habermas' account of communicative action should lead him to merge the aesthetic sphere with a broader sphere of social practices. But because of his commitment to the legacy of aesthetic modernism,

Habermas has been reluctant to abandon a special status for the aesthetic sphere. Albrecht Wellmer, a disciple of Habermas, has attempted to formulate a way of continuing to grant the aesthetic a special status within Habermas' paradigm of communicative reason. I will argue, however, that Wellmer's own criticisms of Adorno's aesthetic theory point to the difficulties of preserving a special status for the aesthetic sphere once one has undermined the metaphysical foundation on which the aesthetic sphere has been built. In order to continue the original aspirations of aesthetic statism, we must now give up on a special metaphysical status for the aesthetic sphere, and allow it to be merged with the larger system of social communication. For that project, Habermas' account of the public sphere and intersubjective communication can provide us with a model of how a nonmetaphysical account of the aesthetic can continue to play a role in social and political formation.

THE CRISIS OF MODERNITY IN "DIALECTIC OF ENLIGHTENMENT"

Robert Hullot-Kentor, Adorno scholar and English translator of Adorno's *Aesthetic Theory*, has asserted that "all of Adorno's writings follow Schiller in conceiving the solution to the dialectic of enlightenment, the realization of reason, as dependent on aesthetic semblance."[2] One could argue that, as a strict issue of intellectual genealogy, Schiller does not seem to have been the most influential figure for Adorno.[3] However, both historically and conceptually, Schiller does stand as the mediator between Kant and Hegel, the two philosophers on whom Adorno focuses intently throughout *Aesthetic Theory*. Thus, viewing Adorno through Schiller opens up significant conceptual continuities in the aesthetic tradition. In discussing Adorno's aesthetic theory, I will begin by stressing the similarities to Schiller's, and then proceed to describe the ways that Adorno's interrogation of the philosophical aesthetic tradition results in a break from Schiller's model of the aesthetic as the unifying sphere for political formation.

Like Schiller's *Aesthetic Letters*, Adorno's *Dialectic of Enlightenment* argues that the subject struggles to resist nature as an imprisoning force.[4] Both Schiller and Adorno follow the Kantian tradition of viewing reason as humankind's means of liberating itself from the forces of nature. But both also argue that reason alone cannot be the sole means of liberation. As I have shown, Schiller criticizes Kant's rationalistic account of the moral law for being rigid and nonsensuous. Adorno similarly criticizes enlightenment instrumental reason for cutting mankind off from a reciprocal relationship with nature, including the fullness of its own human nature. One can also see similarities between Adorno's and Schiller's accounts of the subject's twin determination by nature and reason, what Schiller called the sensuous and the formal drives. According to Schiller, the domination of either drive is detrimental to the balanced development and ultimate freedom of both the individual and humankind as a whole. For Adorno, premodern magic and myth stand for the objective determination by nature, and enlightenment reason stands for rational determination. He likewise argues that either determination alone limits the freedom of the individual. The premodern worldview of magic and myth is limiting because it subordinates human subjectivity to the forces of material nature. The worldview of enlightenment instrumental rationality is limiting because it subordinates material nature, including human nature, to its conceptual and technological control.

Adorno describes the development of enlightenment subjectivity as a process in which, for the sake of survival, individual personality is sacrificed to the general dictates of instrumental reason. The central irony of this kind of sacrifice is underscored in the Odysseus essay in *Dialectic of Enlightenment*. While the sacrifice of one's natural self is supposedly undertaken to preserve one's life against the hostile forces of nature, the subject also sacrifices those natural elements that make life livable: "Man's domination over himself, which grounds his selfhood, is almost always the destruction of the subject in whose service it is undertaken; for the substance which is dominated, suppressed, and dissolved by virtue of self-preservation is none other than that very life as functions of which the achievements of self-preservation find their sole definition and determination" (*DE*, 54–5). The enlightenment sacrifice in the name of human survival thus threatens to become a human sacrifice in a literal sense of that phrase.

The central argument of *Dialectic of Enlightenment* thus presents us with the irony that, while the Enlightenment started as an attempt to reject myth, it ends up reproducing the same limitations as myth. Enlightenment thought reduces material nature to mathematical concepts and formulae. But, instead of acknowledging that these concepts are projected onto nature, enlightenment thought deludes itself into thinking that it has discovered these concepts within nature itself. According to Adorno, this is the same delusion displayed by contemporary philosophic positivism. Enlightenment thought criticizes myths as superstitious structures of projection and repetition, but ends up doing the same thing under the guise of a universally quantifiable science. The categories of enlightenment thought are similarly blind to the real particularity of nature, and, indeed, the real particularity of humankind. It is only through aesthetic experience, Adorno argues, that we can hope to break through the totalizing categories of enlightenment thought and thus catch a glimpse of unassimilated particularity.

UNRECONCILED AESTHETIC RECONCILIATION

For both Schiller and Adorno, aesthetic works are combinations of material and rational elements: "Artworks are, in terms of their own constitution, objective as well as . . . spiritual" (*AT*, 344). Thus they are uniquely situated to overcome the opposition between subject and object: "However much they seem to be entities, artworks are crystallizations of the process between spirit and its other" (*AT*, 344). But, whereas Schiller sees the reconciliation of subjective and objective as already achieved in the aesthetic work, for Adorno the aesthetic work is at best a promissory note of reconciliation. For Adorno, the aesthetic work keeps alive the possibility of this reconciliation of subject and object by retaining traces of those elements that have otherwise been obliterated by the domination of instrumental reason. These are the elements that exist "beyond bourgeois society, its labor, and its commodities," and Adorno often identifies them with natural beauty because it "remains the allegory of this beyond in spite of its mediation through social immanence" (*AT*, 69).

Adorno's assertion that natural beauty is always already mediated through social immanence guards us against a serious misunderstanding of the role of nature for Adorno. When Adorno speaks of recovering traces of oppressed nature in artworks, he is not appealing to a separate, prehuman utopia of nature that we should strive to recover. As he argues in *Dialectic of Enlightenment*, he does not privilege nature *per se* over subjectivity:

Nature herself is neither good, as the ancients believed, nor noble, as the latterday Romantics would have it. As a model and goal it implies the spirit of opposition, deceit, and bestiality. Only when seen for what it is, does nature become existence's craving for peace, that consciousness which from the very beginning has inspired an unshakable resistance to Führer and collective alike. Dominant practice and its inescapable alternatives are not threatened by nature, which tends rather to coincide with them, but by the fact that nature is remembered. *DE*, 254–5

As the last lines of this passage indicate, nature as a domineering force is no better than the Enlightenment as a domineering force. And indeed, in the case of Nazism (never far from Adorno's mind in *Dialectic*), the two readily come together. The Nazis' use of the idea of a naturally pure *Volk* as the proper foundation of the German nation represents a horrific instance of man-made domination attempting to mimic natural domination. The combination of these two forces of domination in Nazism lies behind the bitterly ironic pronouncements in *Dialectic* that enlightenment degenerates into myth and nature.[5]

Either force, subjective rationality or material nature, when left unchecked becomes brutal and domineering. This is why Adorno describes the remembrance of nature, rather than nature itself, as a force for social resistance. Adorno appeals to this memory as a counterforce to the dominant order, the reminder that something once existed and might exist again outside of the system enforced by the dominant order. In the Freudian terms that Adorno sometimes uses, this counterelement of the memory of the other is the only means of limiting the process of projection by which subjectivity creates its perceptual world. Adorno argues that projection is a necessary part of perception, but when projection is left unchecked by any counterforce, subjectivity becomes paranoid and seeks total domination.[6]

For Adorno, the work of art is a microcosm of the same tension between the dominant order and the elements it subordinates. The artwork exhibits a tension between the totalizing force of artistic form and the recalcitrance of the materials upon which this form attempts to impose itself. Thus the political tension between individual and collective is represented in the tensions evident in true art between artistic form and material content. This central importance of tension in the artwork is the basis of Adorno's critique of "the culture industry," and the basis by which he distinguishes true art from the manipulative products of that industry. Adorno's separation of true art from the products of the culture industry has been criticized as a mark of his old-world mandarin aesthetic elitism by defenders of popular culture. My analysis will not enter into the debates concerning specific forms of popular culture, such as American movies and jazz. But, I will argue that Adorno's distinction between true art and the culture industry is not an example of arbitrary elitism, but is rather an essential element of the philosophico-aesthetic project of reconciling the individual and the universal that I have been tracing from Schiller.

According to Adorno, the products of the culture industry strive for an organizing "style" that seamlessly subsumes all particulars within it. Unlike the type of true reconciliation sought in the idealist aesthetic tradition – the reconciliation posited by Schiller's aesthetic sphere or Coleridge's symbol – the products of the culture industry seek to solve the problem of the tension between universal and particular by simply assimilating the particular to the universal and annihilating individual identity in the process. This elimination of the true particular in the products of the culture industry finds its reflection in, and indeed is one of the forces that helps achieve, a corresponding annihilation of true individuality in the modern state as a whole: "The unleashed colossi of the manufacturing industries did not overcome the individual by granting him full satisfaction but by eliminating his character as a subject" (*DE*, 205).

Unlike the products of the culture industry, true art contains an inherent tension between artistic form (style) and the objective materials it attempts to form into a whole. For Adorno, the philosophical and political significance of art emerges precisely from this tension, from the way that artistic form cannot completely assimilate objective materials. This tension thus reflects the crucial assertion of the particularity of the world against the totalizing impulses of artistic form. Like reason, art dominates its materials by transforming them through artistic form, yet successful artworks "rescue over into form something of the amorphous," and "this alone is the reconciling aspect of form" (*AT*, 50).

Adorno thus focuses on the ways in which art is not and cannot ever be seamless, the ways whereby it constantly unravels itself.[7] These are the aspects of Adorno's aesthetics that bear some resemblance to strains of Deconstruction and postmodernist literary criticism, and they are the basis by which Adorno is now being taken up as a forerunner of these types of criticism.[8] But what distinguishes Adorno's aesthetic theory from these contemporary strains of literary criticism is that Adorno's focus on the aesthetic is always undertaken in relation to extra-aesthetic significance. He neither views the unravelling of the artwork as an end in itself, nor as a metaphor for the indeterminacy of all language, but rather as directing us towards truths about the administered world of enlightenment rationality.

Adorno's extra-aesthetic orientation is particularly evident in the emphasis he puts on suffering as a central element of the work of art.

Suffering is central to Adorno's conception of the artwork, because, like the tension of aesthetic form, suffering also indicates the struggle and defeat of those elements dominated by totalizing instrumental reason. Suffering is the result of defeat, but the record of suffering at least preserves the memory of what totalizing reason has sought to annihilate from both experience and thought: "perhaps the most profound force of resistance stored in the cultural landscape is the expression of history that is compelling, aesthetically, because it is etched by the real suffering of the past. The figure of the constrained gives happiness because the force of constraint must not be forgotten; its images are a memento" (*AT*, 64).

Adorno's celebration of this resistance of the particular in the face of totalization thus resembles Coleridge's attempt to retain individuality in the face of the universal in his account of the symbol. But unlike Coleridge and previous philosophical idealism, Adorno is just as concerned with preserving the particularity of the material other of nature as he is with preserving human individuality. And indeed, his argument ultimately is that the one cannot be preserved without preserving the other as well. This deviation from Schiller's and Coleridge's exclusive focus on human subjectivity can be seen in Adorno's central concepts of mimesis and nonidentity, and in his corresponding account of aesthetic reconciliation as "semblance" or "illusion."

For Adorno, mimesis describes nondominating forms of behavior towards, relationships with, and representations of what has been separated from subjectivity as the objective other.[9] Adorno traces mimesis back to primitive human society's relationship to nature, in which, he argues, they attempted to control aspects of nature by imitating its particular properties. This imitative relationship between subject and object in magic is rejected by the development of enlightenment instrumental reason, which attempts to control nature by reducing its particularities to abstract qualities and relationships definable by mathematical equations.[10] Instrumental reason thus seeks a logic of identity, in which everything objective is transformed into reason's abstract concepts. In opposition to this, Adorno posits a logic of nonidentity, in which object particulars refuse assimilation to the totalizing categories of instrumental reason. Along with his philosophical project of negative dialectics, modern art thus represents for Adorno a vital assertion of nonidentity for the modern administered world.

By using the term *mimesis*, Adorno is connecting his concept to an aesthetic tradition that begins with Aristotle's account of imitation in the

Poetics. In the mimesis of primitive societies, magic and art were combined. In the process of modernity, science replaces magic, and art separates itself off from its original use in magical ritual. With the abolition of magical mimetic rituals in the wake of the ascendancy of enlightenment reason as the dominant worldview, art becomes the main repository of mimesis in the modern world. But artistic mimesis means more to Adorno than a process of copying the appearances of the material world. For, according to him, what art imitates is not natural reality *per se*, but natural beauty.

Natural beauty is nature as it appears reconciled with human subjectivity. In his account of natural beauty, Adorno is drawing on the aesthetic concepts of the beautiful and the sublime, particularly as they are enunciated in Kant's *Critique of Judgement*.[11] The beautiful evokes the feeling of a harmony between human subjectivity and nature, while the sublime evokes a feeling of the separation between the two. In these terms, Schiller's account of the aesthetic as I have shown it in the *Aesthetic Letters* is an extended account of the reconciling powers of beauty as applied to the areas of individual and political development.[12]

For Adorno, what he calls artistic "*Schein*" (translated as *semblance* or *illusion*) is the imitation by the artwork of natural beauty, the appearance that art gives of a reconciliation between subject and object. This is the central idea of the idealist aesthetic tradition of Schiller and Coleridge. But Adorno challenges the reality of aesthetic reconciliation claimed by this tradition and proclaimed by traditional art. For him, artistic form is never all-encompassing, and this is precisely art's saving grace. This is what distinguishes it from the totalizing concepts of instrumental reason. According to Adorno, modern art has become self-conscious of its inability to create totally integrated artistic wholes, unlike traditional art's aspirations to total artistic unity. And indeed, modern art self-consciously strives to express the lack of unity of the modern condition.

But modern art is caught in a dilemma. As much as it wants to discard any claim to unity, the very essence of the aesthetic work is aesthetic semblance, the illusionary striving for unity. This is what Adorno means when he speaks of the essentially "affirmative" nature of art. As Albrecht Wellmer describes it in "Truth, Semblance, Reconciliation: Adorno's Aesthetic Redemption of Modernity," the paradoxical dilemma of Adorno's concept of modern art is that "Art can thus only be true in the sense of being faithful to reality to the extent that it shows reality *as* unreconciled, antagonistic, divided against itself. But it can only do this by showing reality in the light of reconciliation, i.e. by the nonviolent aesthetic synthesis of disparate elements which produces the semblance of reconciliation" ("TSR," 9).

THE SEPARATION OF SUBJECTIVE AND AESTHETIC AUTONOMY

Adorno's paradoxical account of modern art's movement towards and against reconciliation has troubling consequences for the role the aesthetic might have for political formation. As I have shown, for the theorists of aesthetic statism, Schiller, Coleridge, and Arnold, the aesthetic sphere is valued for its ability to develop human subjectivity towards a state of freedom and to develop a political state based on such freedom. It is on this basis that the autonomy of the aesthetic sphere is posited and privileged. Because the aesthetic sphere is autonomous from the world of material determination, it provides a medium within which human subjectivity can develop its own, human, autonomy. But it is precisely for focusing exclusively on the aesthetic sphere as a developer of human subjective autonomy that Adorno criticizes the Schillerian aesthetic tradition:

Natural beauty vanished from aesthetics as a result of the burgeoning domination of the concept of freedom and human dignity, which was inaugurated by Kant and then rigorously transplanted into aesthetics by Schiller and Hegel; in accordance with this concept nothing in the world is worthy of attention except that for which the autonomous subject has itself to thank. The truth of such freedom for the subject, however, is at the same time unfreedom: unfreedom for the other. *AT*, 62

For Adorno, the unfree "other" includes both dominated nature and dominated human beings, both of whose suffering art records and preserves from oblivion. But, as one can see here, the other also includes artworks themselves. For Adorno seems to be saying that artworks cannot truly be said to be autonomous if they have as their guiding purpose the cultivation of human ends, even if that end is human freedom itself. Taking this idea within the framework of his critique of the unfreedom of modern society, Adorno's point is that artworks cannot cultivate freedom in an intrinsically unfree world. If they attempted to do so and entered into the realm of instrumental purpose, they would be immediately co-opted by the dominant network of instrumental reason. The only chance artworks have to promote freedom is to stay completely autonomous, to remain a beacon from outside the dominant world of instrumental reason.

Adorno thus argues that artworks are important philosophically and politically by virtue of their very *being*, that is to say, by virtue of their very existence as autonomous entities that keep alive the possibility of reconciliation and freedom. And in keeping with this view, much of *Aesthetic Theory* is devoted to defending the autonomy and separate existence of artworks. As a result of this, in reading *Aesthetic Theory*, one has the odd experience of seeing an aesthetic theory promulgated from what seems like the point of view of the artworks themselves.[13] Some of this sense might come from the fact that, although Adorno discusses literature and, to a lesser extent, the visual arts, music is the form of art that he is most intimately concerned with, and, consequently, music is implicitly the paradigmatic form of art for his aesthetic theory. Being intrinsically nonrepresentational, music lends itself to ideas of existing in its own world.[14]

This returns us to Wellmer's main critique of Adorno: how can the mere existence of artworks that reconcile reason and nature (and even this in a paradoxical manner) serve as mediums of reconciliation for human beings and human society? Given the extreme gap between Adorno's aesthetic world and the world of everyday practice, how is a connection to be made between the two? Wellmer traces this problem in Adorno's aesthetic theory to Adorno's neglect of the communicative function of art. According to Wellmer, Adorno presents aesthetic communication in terms of a model of the perceiving subject adequately apprehending the appearance of reconciliation within the artwork itself, and thus "all that matters is genuinely experiencing works of art and deciphering them philosophically" ("TSR," 16). But, Wellmer objects, there is no exploration in Adorno of the way that artworks speak directly to human beings (the issue of communication and reception) or, furthermore, the way that human beings use artworks to speak to each other (the issue of intersubjective communication). By bringing these issues back into an analysis of the aesthetic, Wellmer thus contrasts a conception of works of art which "point towards an expansion of the boundaries of communication by virtue of their *effect* and not their *being*" ("TSR," 22). In doing so, he is drawing on the work of Habermas, whose theory of intersubjective communicative reason represents a change in paradigm not only for Adorno's aesthetic theory but for critical theory as a whole.

COMMUNICATIVE REASON, THE PUBLIC SPHERE, AND THE *BILDUNG* TRADITION

In *Philosophical Discourse of Modernity*, Habermas argues that, in both Adorno's account of the crisis of modernity in *Dialectic of Enlightenment* and the role of the aesthetic in relation to modernity in *Aesthetic Theory*, Adorno finds himself at the point of aporia, that is to say, in a theoretical position that offers no way out of the contradictions it has uncovered.[15] As I have shown, in *Dialectic of Enlightenment*, Adorno had traced the logic by which instrumental reason extends its dominance over both the external world of nature and the internal world of subjectivity. The faculty of reason that the Enlightenment had thought would provide humankind's liberation turns out instead to be the instrument of humankind's enslavement. Aesthetic works free themselves from the domination of instrumental reason, but at the cost of removing themselves from any tangible connection to actual human social and political practices.

Adorno's philosophy becomes caught in aporia, according to Habermas, because it is constructed according to the paradigm of the philosophy of consciousness, which views questions of knowledge and truth in terms of the relationship between subject and object. Adorno's philosophy finds itself at the point of aporia because Adorno continues to hold on to the fundamental premises of the philosophy of consciousness at the same time that he relentlessly critiques them. But, as Habermas argues, rather than self-consciously remaining within this contradiction, as Adorno does, one should rather take aporia as a signal that one should relinquish the premises that got one there in the first place, namely, the subject/object focus of the philosophy of consciousness:

> Anyone who abides in a paradox on the very spot once occupied by philosophy with its ultimate groundings is not just taking up an uncomfortable position; one can only hold that place if one makes it at least minimally plausible that there is *no way out*. Even the retreat from an aporetic situation has to be barred, for otherwise there is a way – the way back. But I believe this is precisely the case. *PD*, 128

The way back to which Habermas refers is his account of communicative action as the basis of social theory, which changes the central focus of analysis from the relationship between subject and object to the relationship between subject and subject: "the theory of communicative action establishes an internal relation between practice and rationality. It studies the suppositions of rationality inherent in ordinary communicative practice and conceptualizes the normative content of action oriented to mutual understanding in terms of communicative rationality" (*PD*, 76). Habermas explains the history, nuances, and implications of his theory of communicative action in two thick volumes.[16] In addition, whole books and a vast literature of articles in philosophy, political science, and sociology have been devoted to explicating, promoting, or criticizing it. It would not be possible, nor is it my intention, to cover all the major issues brought up by this theory. What I want to do here is examine Habermas' theory of communicative action in terms of a relatively narrow issue, its relationship to the tradition of aesthetic *Bildung* inaugurated by Schiller.

Habermas' stress on intersubjective communication goes back to his early work, and is evident in *The Structural Transformation of the Public Sphere*, a book in which his connection to the *Bildung* tradition is particularly evident. In this work, Habermas describes the public sphere, which reaches the height of its classical form in the eighteenth century, as a sphere of private people coming together as a public in order "to compel public authority to legitimate itself before public opinion" (*ST*, 25). Habermas argues that "the medium of this political confrontation was peculiar and without historical precedent: people's public use of their reason" (*ST*, 27). The overall argument of the book is that the public sphere is essential to an authentic democracy because it makes possible a forum for producing genuine assent among the governed. Habermas critically contrasts the active public debate of engaged citizens in the classical public sphere with the staged legitimation processes of the twentieth century, in which decisions are formed from above and then sold to the modern passive consumer-citizen. Like Arnold's account of the relationship between culture and the state, Habermas' public sphere is both an essential constitutive force of the state, because it is the medium of focusing the individual assent of the citizen, and yet it also remains autonomous from the actual systems of state power.

Habermas identifies culture as one of the central elements that composes the public sphere, and which assists the rational procedures that make political consensus possible. He describes the literary public sphere (*literarische Öffentlichkeit*), and argues that the literary public sphere historically precedes and lays the groundwork for the political public sphere. By the term "literary public sphere," Habermas denotes the eighteenth-century conception of the world of letters, encompassing both nonfiction and fiction, which, for example, is represented in England by both the essays of Addison and the novels of Richardson.

But Habermas' use of the term also includes the central feature of the tradition of aesthetic *Bildung* that I have been tracing from Schiller, namely an autonomous aesthetic sphere that assists in the development of individual subjectivity. It is in this sense that Habermas describes the literary public sphere as providing "the training ground for a critical public reflection still preoccupied with itself – a process of self-clarification of private people focusing on the genuine experiences of their novel privateness" (*PD*, 29).

Habermas' account of the development of music as an autonomous art and its role in developing modern subjectivity shows his connection to the aesthetic tradition we have been tracing from Schiller to Adorno. Habermas argues that until the final years of the eighteenth century all music was "what today we call occasional music": "Judged according to its social function, it served to enhance the sanctity and dignity of worship, the glamor of the festivals at court, and the overall splendor of ceremony." The development of a paying audience for public musical events changed both music and audience:

> Admission for a payment turned the musical performance into a commodity; simultaneously, however, there arose something like music not tied to a purpose. For the first time an audience gathered to listen to music as such . . . Released from its function in the service of social representation, art became an object of free choice and of changing preference. The "taste" to which art was oriented from then on became manifest in the assessments of lay people who claimed no prerogative, since within a public everyone was entitled to judge.
> *PD*, 39-40

Here there are similarities to Adorno's account of the way art becomes autonomous in the process of modernity by freeing itself from its original functions in magical and religious ritual. But whereas Adorno focuses on aesthetic autonomy in terms of the ontological existence of the artworks themselves, Habermas retains Schiller's connection between aesthetic autonomy and the autonomy of the subject. Like Schiller, Habermas' account of the aesthetic sphere in *Structural Transformation* focuses on how it serves as a medium that both develops the individual subject and the political state.

COMMUNICATIVE ACTION AND THE AESTHETIC SPHERE

In *Structural Transformation*, the close connection between the literary and the political public spheres would seem to point towards the centrality of the aesthetic sphere within Habermas' system along the lines of the theories of aesthetic statism that I have been tracing. But as Habermas has developed his system in subsequent works, the aesthetic sphere has not been a central element. And indeed, as I will argue, the way that Habermas has formulated the idea of aesthetic autonomy in his mature work has precluded the aesthetic sphere from occupying a major role in political formation. In *Philosophical Discourse*, Habermas discusses Schiller's *Aesthetic Letters* and asserts that "Schiller stresses the communicative, community-building and solidarity-giving force of art, which is to say, its *public character*" (*PD*, 46; original emphasis). By so characterizing Schiller, Habermas highlights the central connection between the aesthetic sphere and the development of the political state that we have been following in the tradition of aesthetic statism. But Habermas reformulates this connection in terms of a more general model of communication, rather than, as it was for Schiller, in terms of the unique qualities of the aesthetic sphere.

This can be seen in Habermas' further assertion that "Schiller's aesthetic utopia is, however, not aimed at an aestheticization of living conditions, but at revolutionizing the conditions of mutual understanding" (*PD*, 49). In defining Schiller in this way, Habermas is opposing those, like Adorno, who would have the aesthetic sphere supplant reason as the central redeeming element of the philosophical tradition. It is on this ground that he criticizes Adorno's *Aesthetic Theory* for sealing "the surrender of cognitive competency to art" (*PD*, 68). Habermas' position is that, far from being unique, the aesthetic sphere as described by Schiller is a foreshadowing of the potential for intersubjective communication found within ordinary language, as described by Habermas' own theory of communicative action. Contradicting Schiller's concept of the unique autonomy of the aesthetic sphere, Habermas argues that "concealed already in Schiller" is "the idea of the independent logics of the value spheres of science, morality, and art, an idea that would later be worked out energetically by Emil Lask and Max Weber" (*PD*, 50).

Habermas' account of these three independent value spheres is fully expressed in *The Theory of Communicative Action*, and represents a narrowing of the concept of Schiller's autonomous aesthetic sphere and a consequent limiting of its centrality. In *Communicative Action*, Habermas speaks of "autonomous art" and lists it as one of the major developments of the Enlightenment, but what Habermas means by "autonomous" is much more modest philosophically than what Kant, Schiller, and Adorno mean by the same term. Habermas takes his conception of autonomy from Max Weber's account of modernity.[17] For Weber, the process of the rationalization of modern society involves the differentiation of the validity standards of the discourses of science, morality, and aesthetics. These standards had previously been combined in premodern religio-metaphysical worldviews. But in the wake of modernity, each discourse claims its own separate standards for making judgments. This is what Habermas calls a "sphere of validity." Reason has truth for its validity claim; morality has rightness; and aesthetics has beauty.

The discourse of aesthetics is thus autonomous in the sense that the standard for making claims about it, beauty, is different from truth or rightness. In one sense then, aesthetics is just as autonomous as the other two validity spheres of science and morality and should be accorded the same worth.[18] But Habermas' claims in *Communicative Action* for intersubjective consensus depend on the potential universality of discourse claims, and aesthetic judgments according to Habermas are not universalizable. In the case of aesthetic judgments, Habermas argues that "we rely upon the rationally motivating force of the better argument, although a dispute of this kind diverges in a characteristic way from controversies concerning questions of truth and justice" (*TCA*, 42). Habermas thus tries to retain some connection between aesthetic judgment and reason, and in this way he opposes those schools of philosophical positivism which completely separate the two. But, when all is said and done, according to Habermas' own account of rationality, aesthetic arguments cannot be given the same claim to universality that theoretical and moral ones are: "Only in theoretical, practical, and explicative discourse do the participants have to start from the (often counterfactual) presupposition that the conditions for an ideal speech situation are satisfied to a sufficient degree of approximation" (*TCA*, 42). Consequently, aesthetic judgments and arguments cannot be directly integrated within his account of communicative reason.

Because of this, Habermas' account of the aesthetic in *Communicative Action* represents a fundamental break with some of the central features of the Kantian and Schillerian tradition of aesthetics. In describing aesthetic judgments as nonuniversalizable, Habermas breaks with Kant's positing of the universality of the judgment of the beautiful. But even more important for the tradition we have been tracing is the significance of Habermas' account of the "autonomy" of the aesthetic sphere. As I have shown, for Schiller the autonomy of the aesthetic sphere was the unique quality that set it apart from the material and moral spheres. Its autonomy was the basis for bridging the opposition between the other two spheres, and thus conferred on it the central role in the process of individual and political *Bildung*. But what special role can the aesthetic sphere have, if it is just one autonomous sphere among several, and one whose judgments are not even potentially universalizable?

THE AESTHETIC SPHERE AND COMMUNICATIVE ACTION

In *Philosophical Discourse*, Habermas had argued that, by focusing so centrally on aesthetic experience, Adorno had given up on the enlightenment commitment to reason as the vehicle of social critique and progress. But the scant role that the aesthetic plays in *Communicative Action* opens Habermas up to the opposite charge that, as Hullot-Kentor expresses it, by denying the unique centrality of the aesthetic sphere, it is rather Habermas who separates himself from the tradition of the Enlightenment, specifically Kant and Schiller, for whom "aesthetics becomes the key to the recuperation of reason."[19] In reaction to this sort of criticism, in some of his writings since *The Theory of Communicative Action*, Habermas has sought to formulate a more robust role for the aesthetic sphere and to thereby reconnect himself to the aesthetic strain of enlightenment philosophy and specifically to Adorno's defense of aesthetic modernism.[20] In discussing the limited role of aesthetic discourse in *Communicative Action*, Habermas has argued that the account there applies only to the discourse *about* aesthetic works (i.e., criticism), not to the works themselves.[21] Habermas has thus tried to defend himself from the charge that his system fails to recognize the special importance of aesthetic works.

The details of working out the role of aesthetic works within the framework of Habermas' philosophy have, however, largely been undertaken by one his disciples, Albrecht Wellmer, whose critiques of Adorno I mentioned at the end of chapter 2. In his essay "Truth, Semblance, Reconciliation," Wellmer has sought to define the importance of the aesthetic sphere within the paradigm of communicative reason. Overall, Wellmer supports Adorno's defense of the political value of aesthetic modernism, but criticizes the separation from social communication entailed by Adorno's account of aesthetic autonomy. Wellmer seeks to connect the aesthetic sphere to the positive, nontotalizing, political traditions of the Enlightenment that Habermas has sought to uncover and formulate in his account of a noncoercive public sphere. In the same way that Habermas identified Schiller's aesthetic sphere as a forerunner of the theory of communicative action, Wellmer argues that Habermas' account of intersubjective communication presupposes that "a mimetic moment is sublated in everyday speech, just as it is in art and philosophy" ("TSR," 13).

Wellmer contrasts this approach with Adorno's account, which, he argues, "can only conceive mimesis as the other of rationality, and the coming-together of mimesis and rationality only as the negation of historical reality" ("TSR," 13). Because Adorno's utopian projection of the aesthetic sphere is "the other of discursive reason," it exists in another world. But because Habermas' project is rooted in the conditions of everyday linguistic practice, "the utopia is of this world" ("TSR," 14) and thus potentially achievable. Wellmer thus argues that Habermas' account of communicative action fulfills the mediating function previously ascribed to the aesthetic sphere: "If we think of unimpaired intersubjectivity as a condition which permits a multiplicity of subjects to come together without coercion, making it possible for individuals to exist at one and the same time in proximity and distance, in identity and diversity, then this represents a utopian projection constructed by discursive reason out of elements that are rooted in the nature of language" ("TSR," 14).

But the consequence of this and Wellmer's previous assertion that "a mimetic moment is sublated in everyday speech, just as it is in art and philosophy" ("TSR," 13), is to call into doubt the need for a special category of the aesthetic. On this account, mimesis, the special defining feature of art for Adorno, is absorbed into the broader category of intersubjective communication. And this in turn makes it difficult to appeal to the unique value of avant-garde art, as Wellmer does when he asserts that "without aesthetic experience and the subversive potential it contains, our moral discourse would necessarily become blind and our interpretations of the world empty" ("TSR," 34). For, as we saw in Adorno's defense of aesthetic modernism, the defense of such "subversive" artistic practices goes hand in hand with a rejection of the adequacy of ordinary language to accurately portray reality. Indeed, Adorno's defense of artistic modernism is intrinsically connected to the philosophical argument that the system of ordinary language is part of a totalizing system that oppresses the individual. But following Habermas, Wellmer is supposed to be defending the structure of ordinary language as a vehicle of political emancipation.

By identifying ordinary language with the totalizing system of enlightenment reason, Adorno had given his version of this argument a particularly political inflection, but the basic idea is evident in other theoretical proponents of aesthetic modernism such as Hulme, Beckett, and Proust.[22] Ultimately this idea can be traced back to the central Romantic paradigm of the subject who undertakes a quest to grasp the true nature of reality, and who seeks and creates new forms of art, language, and experience in the process. In short, the traditional defense of modern art is connected to the very philosophy of consciousness model that Habermas and Wellmer are seeking to escape from. The very strength that Habermas' intersubjective model has for banishing the aporias of the philosophy of consciousness also banishes the traditional theoretical defenses of avant-garde art.

A POSTMETAPHYSICAL AESTHETICS

In reviewing and contrasting the role of the aesthetic in Adorno, Habermas, and Wellmer, one can see that a theory of aesthetic statism in the twentieth century faces the following dilemma. It can continue to claim a special status for the aesthetic sphere based on aesthetic autonomy, but in doing so it risks losing connection with and thus influence on the social and political world. This is the position that Adorno's aesthetic theory occupies. On the other hand, a theory of aesthetic statism can relinquish the claim for a special status for the aesthetic sphere and allow the aesthetic sphere to be absorbed into the broader system of social practices, but in doing so it risks losing the advantage of being able to criticize the system of social practices from the outside. This second position is, I would argue, what Habermas' account of communicative action logically leads to. But, as I have indicated, because of the risk of losing the emancipatory claims of aesthetic modernism, Habermas and Wellmer attempt to retain a special status for the aesthetic sphere, with the attendant contradictions I have noted above.

Given these two basic choices, my position is that the second alternative holds out the best chance of retaining and fulfilling the original aspirations of aesthetic statism. I would argue, therefore, that rather than attempting to hold on at all costs and all theoretical contradiction to the special separate status of the aesthetic sphere, it is time to allow it to be seen as part of the broader system of social practices. I will further maintain that one can do this and still retain the sort of emancipatory power that aesthetic statism previously ascribed to an autonomous aesthetic sphere. According to this new perspective, the locus of this emancipatory power would be shifted from the aesthetic sphere *per se* towards a larger conception of culture connected to the public sphere.

At this point, one might question, however, whether anything would remain of the tradition of aesthetic statism, if one were to relinquish the special autonomy and special status of the aesthetic sphere. In order to address this overall question, it is necessary to examine the following questions in order: Why should one relinquish the special category and status of the aesthetic sphere? What are the consequences of merging the aesthetic sphere with the broader sphere of social and cultural practices? And finally, how can the emancipatory power previously attributed to the aesthetic sphere be retained without a special metaphysical category and status?

Why should the special status for the aesthetic be relinquished? As I have shown in reviewing the concept of aesthetic autonomy from Schiller through Adorno, this special status is explicitly or tacitly based on metaphysical premises whose validity can no longer be defended from the perspective of contemporary theory. But even if one were to leave theoretical objections aside, I would argue that, from a purely pragmatic perspective, the special separate status of the aesthetic sphere, particularly as it has been formulated in most of twentieth-century literary theory, no longer furthers the original goal of aesthetic statism, which was to promote individual freedom in the face of totalizing forces. The concept of aesthetic autonomy has been transformed into the indeterminacy of literary discourse, and I began this book precisely by questioning the way in which the indeterminacy of literary works has been celebrated as an end-in-itself by critical approaches from New Criticism through Deconstruction through what is now called postmodernism. From the standpoint of the enlightenment project of individual freedom, such accounts of literary indeterminacy, at best, lead to apolitical aesthetic formalism. At worst, literary indeterminacy has been enlisted in the cause of philosophical projects seeking to deconstruct individual subjectivity.

What are the consequences of merging the aesthetic sphere with the broader sphere of social and cultural practices? Doesn't doing this precisely give up the emancipatory power of the aesthetic sphere for the development of individual freedom and cast us at the mercy of cultural nationalism or totalitarianism? This danger, as I have argued, is the reason that Habermas and Wellmer are reluctant to give up on the special status of the aesthetic sphere. Following the terms laid out by

Adorno's critique of modernity, they want to be able to keep a strict categorical separation between true art, with its emancipatory potential, and the products of the culture industry, with their complicity with global totalizing systems. As I have shown, the argument is that in order to resist such totalizing systems, the aesthetic sphere has to be in some sense outside of or autonomous from them.

But as a practical matter, how does one determine which works have this resistance to the system? Adorno posits an *ontological* difference, that is to say, a difference in terms of the essential inner constitution of the artwork itself. What defines the true artwork is the constitutive tension between its artistic form and the recalcitrant materials that it seeks to organize within this form. Its own inner constitution is a reflection of its struggle against totalization. But as I have shown, Habermas and Wellmer reject this ontological paradigm in favor of a paradigm defined through communication and reception. They define the artwork not in terms of its own inner being, but in terms of its intended meaning and its effect on its audience.

I agree that this is absolutely the right paradigm to adopt if one wants to connect aesthetic works to the public sphere. But because Habermas and Wellmer both continue to connect the emancipatory potential of the aesthetic with Adorno's account of modern art, they also continue to seek a way of defining a categorical difference for aesthetic works. I have given my account of how I think this entails theoretical contradictions for their system. But waiving for the moment the question of theoretical contradiction, I would argue that even from a purely pragmatic standpoint, there is no benefit to be gained by insisting on such a formal categorical difference within the theory of communicative action. Indeed, the way that Habermas and Wellmer define a special category for aesthetic works has the reverse effect of undermining the influence that aesthetic works could have on the public sphere, because the speech-act propositional/non-propositional approach they must adopt to retain the categorical distinction is ultimately unhelpful in providing a way of discussing aesthetic works in terms of the central issue of human freedom. Habermas' approach to aesthetic discourse in *Communicative Action* is based on speech-act philosophy and pragmatic linguistics, and following in these traditions takes as its central question the propositional truth value of works of art. This approach defines the specialness of aesthetic discourse in terms of fictive speech. The basic argument, which is reminiscent to students of literary criticism of I. A. Richards' theory of literary "pseudostatements," is that, as fictive speech, aesthetic discourse does not intend to present verifiable propositional statements.

While it is true that such a speech-act approach provides a basis for distinguishing a separate category of aesthetic works, such an approach gives up the key distinction that informed Adorno's distinction between true art and products of the culture industry in the first place. For, from the standpoint of a speech-act analysis of discourse, the most cynically manipulative product of the culture industry qualifies as aesthetic discourse just as much as any true work of art in Adorno's canon. Namely, both are examples of "fictive speech," both do not intend referential propositional statements, and so on. If one wants to continue to make Adorno's type of distinction between emancipatory art and controlling cultural commodity, one cannot do it on these or on any other purely formal categorical grounds. Instead, one has to proceed by analysis of the particular work in question in relation to social contexts, rather than by the presupposition of a special general category of the aesthetic. Thus in order to distinguish works into one or the other camp, one has to make a case for each individual work by providing a social reading. And indeed, I would argue that even Adorno's avowedly ontological accounts of works of art gain their persuasiveness from Adorno's readings of the relationships between the formal particulars of individual works of art within their social contexts. Since one has to make the case work-by-work anyway, nothing is really lost in giving up a special ontological or formal category for aesthetic works. And something is gained in the sense that a more fluid relationship is revealed between the categories of "true aesthetic work" and "cultural commodity." Indeed, one of the central insights of cultural studies has been to argue that even works that are produced for all the wrong reasons (in Adorno's sense) as cultural commodities can in certain contexts have the same kind of emancipatory potential as Adorno's ontologically true artworks.

But how can the emancipatory power previously attributed to the aesthetic sphere be retained without a special metaphysical category and status? The short answer is that the emancipatory power previously attributed to an autonomous aesthetic sphere should rather be understood in terms of a broader model of culture in relation to the public sphere. What I am sketching here is a socially interactive conception of culture, like Habermas' account of the literary public sphere in *Structural Transformation*. In this sense, the central impulse of Habermas' account of the public sphere recalls Coleridge's central project of "enunciating the whole," the reconciliation of particular and universal in a political structure. But instead of being based on the special nature of the symbol, Habermas bases it on the dialectical interaction between particular and universal implicit in the possibility of language itself. This recalls a central element of Schiller's model of the aesthetic sphere, that the aesthetic work is an objective entity as formed by human subjectivity. It is the universal as recapitulated through individual subjectivity.

Charles Taylor's account of Habermas' theory of communicative action presents a useful explanation of this central idea as it applies to general linguistic theory. Taylor describes the complementarity between linguistic structure and practice:

> A language can be understood as a structure or as a code. This code is normative for speech acts. Yet, the relation between structure and act is not one-sided in that the former exists only because it is continually renewed in linguistic practice. In other words, a reciprocal relationship obtains between structure and practice, or, to use Saussure's terms, between "langue and parole," preventing the one side of the relation being reduced to the other. We do not create the structure in our respective speech acts, for these presuppose the existence of that code; but the structure survives only in those acts and reproduces itself in them – thus persisting in the form of ceaseless mutation.[23]

Taylor describes the two central ways in which language is viewed, and how the two are complementary. On the one hand, language is viewed as a *structure*, that is to say, as a collective set of rules and practices that dictate the form of any individual speech act (Saussure's *langue*). On the other hand, language is viewed in terms of the *linguistic practice of individuals*, the actual speech acts of individuals in the world (Saussure's *parole*). Taylor argues that the traditional debates about the priority of structure or practice are misguided, because the two aspects of language are intrinsically connected. A language without a general structure would have no individual speech acts. But, conversely, without individual speech acts there would also be no language.

What Taylor is describing in terms of linguistic theory parallels the distinction I have discussed between cultural nationalism and individualistic liberalism in political theory. As I have shown, in cultural nationalism, the individual is seen as a particular embodiment of the collective common culture. Individualistic liberalism, in contrast, begins with the uniqueness of the individual subject. Taylor describes the consequences of this analogy between linguistic and political theory:

> One would think that it would have been obvious to apply this structure/practice principle to a theory of society. Yet it has in reality always been

neglected. Most thinkers, such as Hegel and Herder, defended the first, fundamentalist approach, namely the originality of community, and thus paid a certain amount of attention to the S/P principle. However, the principle more or less went overboard in the reception of the fundamentalist approach in French sociology, from Saint-Simon and Comte to Durkheim. Durkheim therefore offers us a non-atomistic theory of society, stating that there are non-reducible "faits sociaux," without, however, paying any heed to the second approach, namely the S/P principle. "Language and Society," 24

Now, the projects of aesthetic statism I examined had as their goal precisely a reconciliation of individual subjectivity and collective social practice based on the unique role of the aesthetic. For Taylor, the reconciliation is based on heeding the "S/P principle," that is, the complementarity between social structure and practice. In his reply to Taylor, Habermas expands on this idea:

I want to make a point which Wilhelm von Humboldt brought up . . . For Humboldt already conceives of reaching understanding as a mechanism which *socializes* and *individuates* in one act. In the structure of diffracted intersubjectivity – which demands of the competent speaker that he or she master the system of personal pronouns – singularization is just as impossible without the inexorable compulsion to universalization as is socialization without concomitant individuation. "Questions and Counterquestions," 218

Habermas has expanded on this model of intersubjective communication as a process that simultaneously socializes and individuates in two recent essays, "The Unity of Reason in the Diversity of its Voices" and "Individuation Through Socialization: On George Herbert Mead's Theory of Subjectivity."[24]

In making his appeal for retaining the idea of a unity in reason, Habermas has retained the centrality of individual improvement of the *Bildung* tradition. For, he argues, without some concept of a unity of reason among all its various cultural forms, there would be no way that we could "improve our own standards of rationality" ("Unity of Reason," 137). Habermas appeals to the model of conversational interaction to make this point. We would never enter into a conversation with someone whose views differed from ours unless we thought that learning from the other was at least a possibility. How could we have any expectation of learning from someone else if we did not implicitly hold the idea of a possible common ground of reason? Expanding this analogy, Habermas argues that the same potential must exist for the dialogue across different cultures as it does between different individuals. Particular languages, he argues, "present themselves as individual totalities and yet are porous to one another" ("Individuation Through Socialization," 163). And while "languages impress their own stamp on world-views and forms of life and thus make translations from one language into others more difficult," nonetheless "they are directed like converging rays towards the common goal of reaching universal understanding" (163). Habermas thus appeals to a nontotalizing account of shared rationality as the necessary presupposition of the possibility of reaching consensus between both individuals and cultural nations.

As one can see in these summaries of Habermas' attempts to construct a compelling postmetaphysical model of the dialectic relationship between individual and universal, what takes the reconciling role of the aesthetic sphere is the universality of basic forms of intersubjective speech acts. Habermas' appeal is towards an increasingly universal ground of agreement based on a model of commonality within and between language communities. This represents the specifically linguistic turn in his work since *The Structural Transformation of the Public Sphere*, and the technical nature of his working out his model of pragmatic linguistics makes some of this work less accessible to a wider humanistic audience. But in concluding, I would stress the continuity between his earlier account of the public sphere and these more recent attempts to provide an account of reaching understanding as a process which "socializes and individuates in one act." For this also describes the role of culture as it is presented in his earlier account of the development of the public sphere, and provides a useful understanding of the role a postmetaphysical account of culture can continue to play in relation to the public sphere.

As I have shown, according to Habermas' account in chapter 7 of *Structural Transformation*, the subjectivity developed in the literary public sphere lays the groundwork for the political public sphere. I would argue that this provides a model of the development of individual, rather than atomistically individualistic, subjectivity. This is the model I would urge for culture, that it raises one's consciousness, not in order to break from the community, which is cultural nationalism's fear of liberalism, but to enter into that community by making it one's own, through the process of individual acceptance. Just as Taylor and Habermas assert the reciprocity between linguistic structure and practice, so too, echoing Arnold's connection of culture with freedom, I would assert that culture is not the monolithic determiner of consciousness posited by the cultural nationalist. Culture only exists because it is internalized and then reproduced by individuals who, in the act of reproducing it, inevitably change it in accordance with their individuality.

By reintegrating this concept of individual subjectivity within the concept of the cultural nation, one can find connections between what threaten to become isolated cultural monads. The point is not to connect by abstracting from the specificity of culture, but to self-consciously work through that specificity, first with one's own set of cultural connections, and then to work out to others. This, it seems to me, is what usefully remains of the tradition of aesthetic statism once one removes the metaphysical and traditionalist elements that are no long plausible or defensible from our contemporary perspective. It may no longer constitute a metaphysical theory, but it represents a regulative ideal that still beckons to us forcibly.

Notes

INTRODUCTION

1 Jerome J. McGann, *The Romantic Ideology* (University of Chicago Press, 1983), 48.
2 Richard Rorty, "The Priority of Democracy to Philosophy," in *Objectivity, Relativism, and Truth: Philosophical Papers Volume I* (Cambridge University Press, 1991), 193–4.
3 Ernesto Laclau and Chantal Mouffe, *Hegemony and Socialist Strategy*, trans. Winston Moore and Paul Cammack (London: Verso, 1985).
4 Raymond Williams in *Culture and Society, 1780–1950* (New York: Columbia University Press, 1983) gives the classic account of the relationship between aesthetics and politics throughout nineteenth-century England, and my work proceeds from the pioneering basis he lays there. I also draw on the recent neo-Marxist cultural studies of David Lloyd: "Arnold, Ferguson, Schiller: Aesthetic Culture and the Politics of Aesthetics," *Cultural Critique*, vol. 1, no. 2 (Winter 1985), 137–69; *Nationalism and Minor Literature* (Berkeley: University of California Press, 1987), 137–69; and *Anomalous States* (Durham, N.C.: Duke University Press, 1993).
5 De Man's analysis is in "The Rhetoric of Temporality," in *Blindness and Insight*, 2nd edn. (Minneapolis: University of Minnesota Press, 1983), 187–228. For a review of deconstructionist readings of Coleridge's account of the symbol and a critique of their limitations, see Steven Knapp, *Personification and the Sublime: Milton to Coleridge* (Cambridge, Mass: Harvard University Press, 1985), esp. 150–1, notes 15–17.
6 A renewed interest in this work might be signaled and initiated by the publication of the new edition of *Culture and Anarchy* (1994) in the Yale "Rethinking the Western Tradition" series, edited by Samuel Lipman with new interpretive essays by Maurice Cowling, Gerald Graff, Samuel Lipman, and Steven Marcus. Of these essays, Graff's is the best at connecting Arnold's concerns with the issues of cultural criticism as they develop in the twentieth century. The critic who focuses most substantially on the issue of the state is Lipman, but he does so mainly in the context of recounting neoconservative objections to the growth of state power in this century.

7 The way for such an analysis has been prepared by the emergence in the past decade of political and new historical studies in Romanticism, such as: Marilyn Butler, *Romantics, Rebels and Reactionaries: English Literature and its Background, 1760–1830* (Oxford University Press, 1982); Jerome J. McGann, *The Romantic Ideology* (University of Chicago Press, 1983); James Chandler, *Wordsworth's Second Nature* (University of Chicago Press, 1984); Marjorie Levinson, *Wordsworth's Great Period Poems* (Cambridge University Press, 1986); David Simpson, *Wordsworth's Historical Imagination* (London: Methuen, 1987), and *Romanticism, Nationalism, and the Revolt Against Theory* (University of Chicago Press, 1993); Nigel Leask, *The Politics of Imagination in Coleridge's Critical Thought* (London: Macmillan, 1988); Alan Liu, *Wordsworth: The Sense of History* (Stanford University Press, 1989); and Frederick C. Beiser, *Enlightenment, Revolution, and Romanticism* (Cambridge, Mass: Harvard University Press, 1992). James Chandler's *England 1819* (University of Chicago Press, 1989) is a sustained attempt to explicate what a historicist approach entails for Romanticism studies in particular and cultural studies in general. As will be evident from my comments below in the "Motivations" section of this introduction, I particularly agree with Chandler's analysis (135–40) of how the "return-to-history" movement in Romanticism studies has tended to ignore or dismiss the theories of history expressed by Romantic texts themselves.

8 Williams, *Culture and Society*. Josef Chytry, *The Aesthetic State: A Quest in Modern German Thought* (Berkeley: University of California Press, 1989).

9 See Chytry, *Aesthetic State*, chapter 6, "The *Aufhebung* of the Aesthetic State," esp. 204–5.

1 MODERNITY, SUBJECTIVITY, LIBERALISM, AND NATIONALISM

1 Raymond Williams, *Culture and Society, 1780–1950* (New York: Columbia University Press, 1983), 62.

2 M. H. Abrams, *Natural Supernaturalism* (New York: Norton, 1973), 443.

3 The issue of early and late in the careers of Wordsworth and Coleridge enters into this as well. It becomes convenient to cut off the later careers of these two figures as non-Romantic, even though their later work is fully continuous with their early work. The onus should be on critics to demonstrate where the great rupture comes that renders their later work non-Romantic, and to explain by what basis that judgment is made.

4 Thus when Hartman wants to make a general case for the importance of Wordsworth, he makes it by pointing to Wordsworth's "affinity to the great European Romantics – to Rousseau, Hölderlin, Hegel." Geoffrey Hartman, *Wordsworth's Poetry, 1787–1814* (Cambridge, Mass.: Harvard University Press, 1987), xxv.

5 Paul de Man, "The Rhetoric of Temporality," in *Blindness and Insight*, 2nd edn. (Minneapolis: University of Minnesota Press, 1983), 187–228.

6 Marilyn Butler, "Plotting the Revolution: The Political Narrative of Romantic Poetry and Criticism," in *Romantic Revolutions*, ed. Kenneth

Johnston, et al. (Bloomington: Indiana University Press, 1990), 133–57: 134.

7 The English tradition of opposing theory has recently been explored in David Simpson's *Romanticism, Nationalism, and the Revolt Against Theory* (University of Chicago Press, 1993).

8 For a thorough examination of this, see Josef Chytry's discussion in *The Aesthetic State: A Quest in Modern German Thought* (Berkeley: University of California Press, 1989) chapter 4, esp. 123–35, of Hegel, Hölderin and Schelling's collaborative work, *The Earliest Systemprogram of German Idealism*.

9 Carl Woodring, *Politics in English Romantic Poetry* (Cambridge, Mass.: Harvard University Press, 1970), 26.

10 This is the basis on which a theorist of nationalism like Elie Kedourie argues that nationalist thought originates in the Kantian tradition of autonomous subjectivity. See *Nationalism* (London: Hutchinson, 1966).

11 *RG*, 374.

12 Every form of polity, every condition of society, whatever else it had done, had formed its type of national character ... Accordingly, the views respecting the various elements of human culture and the causes influencing the formation of national character, which pervade the writings of the Germano-Coleridgian school, throw into the shade everything which had been effected before, or which has been attempted simultaneously by any other school. Such views are, more than anything else, the characteristic feature of the Goethian period of German literature; and are richly diffused through the historical and critical writings of the New French school, as well as of Coleridge and his followers." (John Stuart Mill, *Mill on Bentham and Coleridge* [London: Chatto & Windus, 1967], 132–133).

Earlier in the essay Mill identifies this school of historicism with "that series of great writers and thinkers, from Herder to Michelet" (131).

13 "The state therefore is not a collection of individuals who have come together in order to protect their own particular interests; the state is higher than the individual and comes before him." Kedourie, *Nationalism*, 38.

14 It is sometimes argued that there are two or more varieties of nationalism, the linguistic being only one of a number, and the Nazi doctrine of race is brought forward to illustrate the argument that there can be racial, religious, and other nationalisms. But, in fact, there is no definite clear-cut distinction between linguistic and racial nationalism. Originally, the doctrine emphasized language as the test of nationality, because language was an outward sign of a group's particular identity and a significant means of ensuring its continuity. But a nation's language was peculiar to that nation only because such a nation constituted a racial stock distinct from that of other nations." Kedourie, *Nationalism*, 71–2.

15 "We can distinguish an early period in which nations have a more plantlike, impersonal existence and growth and a later period in which the consciousness will of the nation awakens. In this later period ... the nation becomes aware of itself as a great personality, as a great historical unit, and it now lays claim to self-determination, the mark and privilege of

the mature personality." Friedrich Meinecke, *Cosmopolitanism and the National State*, trans. Robert B. Kimber (Princeton University Press, 1970), 12.

Thus Friedrich Schlegel called for the autonomy of the state's personality: "Every state is an independently existing individual. It is completely its own master, has its own particular character, and governs itself according to its own particular laws, customs, and usages." Quoted in Meinecke, *Cosmopolitanism*, 68.

16 For Adam Müller the state must reach a point at which "private life is nothing but national life seen from below and public life, in the last analysis, nothing but that same national life seen from above," and nationality is "the divine harmony, reciprocity, and interaction between private and public interests." Quoted in Meinecke, *Cosmopolitanism*, 103 and 111.

17 "What is beyond doubt is that the doctrine divides humanity into separate and distinct nations, claims that such nations must constitute sovereign states, and asserts that the members of a nation reach freedom and fulfillment by cultivating the peculiar identity of their own nation and by sinking their own persons in the greater whole of the nation." Kedourie, *Nationalism*, 73.

18 Hagen Schulze, *The Course of German Nationalism: From Frederick the Great to Bismark 1763–1867*, trans. Sarah Hanbury-Tenison (Cambridge University Press, 1991), 43.

19 For accounts of the English state and the constitution see J. G. A. Pocock, *The Ancient Constitution and the Feudal Law. A Reissue with Retrospective* (Cambridge University Press, 1987); J. G. A. Pocock, *The Machiavellian Moment: Florentine Political Thought and the Atlantic Republican Tradition* (Princeton University Press, 1975); J. G. A. Pocock, "Burke and the Ancient Constitution," in *Politics, Language, and Time* (New York: Atheneum, 1971); and Corinne Comstock Weston, *English Constitutional Theory and the House of Lords, 1556–1832* (London: Routledge & Kegan Paul, 1965).

20 Gerald Newman, *The Rise of English Nationalism: A Cultural History, 1740–1830* (New York: St. Martin's, 1987); Linda Colley, *Britons: Forging the Nation, 1707–1837* (New Haven: Yale University Press, 1992).

21 "Politically and especially in view of their strident patriotism . . . Wordsworth and the repentant Lake Poets may appear 'reactionary' to observers today; Byron and his friends may, for opposite reasons, appear 'liberal.' But *socially* (and this was really the more important dimension), it was Wordsworth and his friends who were the true radicals, and Byron and his who were the aristocratic reactionaries of contemporary letters." Newman, *Rise of English Nationalism*, 242.

22 Frederick C. Beiser, *Enlightenment, Revolution, and Romanticism: The Genesis of Modern German Political Thought, 1790–1800* (Cambridge, Mass.: Harvard University Press, 1992).

23 Hannah Arendt, *Lectures on Kant's Political Philosophy*, edited and with an interpretive essay by Ronald Beiner (University of Chicago Press, 1982).

24 Immanuel Kant, *Idea for a Universal History with a Cosmopolitan Purpose*, in Hans Reiss, ed., *Kant's Political Writings* (Cambridge University Press, 1970), 45. For an extensive discussion of Kant's liberalism, see Beiser, *Enlightenment, Revolution, and Romanticism*, 27–56.
25 "In man (as the only rational creature on earth), *those natural capacities which are directed towards the use of his reason are such that they could be fully developed only in the species, but not in the individual*" (Kant's italics). *Idea for a Universal History*, 42.
26 As we will see below in chapter 3, Schiller also uses separate terms to eliminate this ambiguity when necessary.
27 See Josef Chytry, *The Aesthetic State: A Quest in Modern German Thought* (Berkeley: University of California Press, 1989), 92, in which he argues that Schiller uses the Greek model, but seeks to surpass it in terms of self-conscious freedom.
28 The backwardness of Germany becomes an issue for the Marxist tradition because, according to Marx, ideology is a reflection of the modes of production of a nation. How then could Germany, which was backwards in the processes of modernization compared to England and France, have produced a philosophical system like Hegel's which so clearly defined in ideological form the crises of modernity. Lukacs' *The Young Hegel* (Cambridge, Mass.: MIT Press, 1976) focuses on this problem.
29 Richard Rorty, "The Priority of Democracy to Philosophy," in *Philosophical Papers*, vol. 1 (Cambridge University Press, 1991), 184.

2 THE SYMBOL AND THE AESTHETIC SPHERE

1 New Criticism regarded such symbolic language as the essence of poetry, and this accounts for their attacks on the "heresy of paraphrase": "The poem communicates so much and communicates it so richly and with such delicate qualifications that the thing communicated is mauled and distorted if we attempt to convey it by any vehicle less subtle than that of the poem itself." Cleanth Brooks, *The Well Wrought Urn* (New York: Harcourt Brace Jovanovich, 1947), 72–3.
2 Walter Benjamin, *The Origin of German Tragic Drama*, trans. John Osborne (London: New Left Books, 1977), 159-60.
3 See Frank Lentricchia, *After the New Criticism* (University of Chicago Press, 1980).
4 But not every dialectical theorist explicitly foregrounds the symbol in their philosophical system. See my comments on Chytry's analysis of Hegel in the introduction, and note 8 on Hegel below.
5 The exact relationship of Hegel's dialectic to actually existing reality remains a vexed interpretive question. Hegel is often seen as connecting the movement of the dialectic with the actual course of human history; this is an aspect of Hegel associated with his *Lectures on the Philosophy of History*, an aspect stressed by the Marxist tradition. On the other hand, a

contrasting element in Hegel's writings is the way that Spirit progresses by emancipating itself from the limitations of physical forms. In Hegel's *Aesthetics*, art advances spiritually as it becomes less tied to physical forms. And indeed, in Hegel's philosophical system, art remains at a lower level than philosophy, precisely because even the most subjectively advanced art remained tied to some sort of material form. (For a discussion of these issues see Robert Pippin, *Hegel's Idealism* [Cambridge University Press, 1989] esp. 3-15, and James H. Wilkinson, "On Hegel's Project," *British Journal for the History of Philosophy* 2, no. 1, 1994, 87–144.)

6   Coleridge actually read a bit of Hegel, but, ironically, was not particularly impressed, and certainly did not see him as the culmination of German Idealism. Coleridge's marginalia on Hegel have been published in the second volume of the Collected Works edition of the *Marginalia*. G. N. G. Orsini, *Coleridge and German Idealism* (Carbondale: Southern Illinois University Press, 1969), 242–5 describes Coleridge's other passing references to Hegel.

7   This formulation from *Church and State* (1830) is a condensed version of Coleridge's analysis in essays 8 and 9 of *The Essays on Method* in which he attempts to bring the idealism of Plato together with the Natural Science of Bacon (see *The Friend*, vol. 1, 482–95). For an account of Coleridge's ideas of Natural Science, see Owen Barfield, *What Coleridge Thought* (Middletown, Conn.: Wesleyan University Press, 1971), chapter 2, "Naturata and Naturans."

8   Hegel in his various dialectical reconciliations of universal and particular has many elements that work like symbols: the ancient polis and the "plastic" work of art of ancient Greece, the Incarnation, and the State of *The Philosophy of Right*. But Hegel's emphasis in his philosophy is on "Spirit" rather than the symbol *per se*. The reason for Hegel's lack of emphasis of the symbol is connected to the role art plays in his mature system of philosophy. As is well known, for Hegel, art comes beneath philosophy in the progression of the dialectic. Habermas describes the limitations Hegel saw in even the most subjectively advanced art, what Hegel called Romantic art: "Romanticism is the 'completion' [*Vollendung*] of art both in the sense of a subjectivistic disintegration of art into reflection and in the sense of a reflective penetration of a form of presentation of the absolute still tied down to the symbolic" (*PD*, 35). But even in Romantic art, the residue of a material substratum required by the very nature of symbolism makes art a less pure vehicle for thought than philosophy for Hegel.

9   For background on Coleridge on Reason and Understanding, see Owen Barfield, *What Coleridge Thought*, chapters 8 and 9. For Coleridge's relation to and differences from Kant's use of these terms, see Orsini, *Coleridge and German Idealism*, 83–4 and 140–1.

10 See Thomas McFarland, "The Origin and Significance of Coleridge's Theory of Secondary Imagination," in Geoffrey Hartman, ed., *New*

Perspectives on Coleridge and Wordsworth (New York: Columbia University Press, 1972), 13.

11 See Hans W. Frei, *The Eclipse of Biblical Narrative: A Study in Eighteenth- and Nineteenth-Century Hermeneutics* (New Haven: Yale University Press, 1974).

12 See chapter 1, note 8 above, and *PD*, 88ff.

13 For a fuller discussion of the background of the Higher Biblical Criticism in relation to *The Statesman's Manual*, see my "The Incarnated Symbol: Coleridge, Hegel, Strauss, and the Higher Biblical Criticism," *European Romantic Review*, vol. 4, no. 2, Winter 1994, 133–50. For more comprehensive studies treating Coleridge's theology in relation to the Higher Biblical Criticism, see Elinor S. Shaffer, *"Kubla Khan" and "The Fall of Jerusalem"* (Cambridge University Press, 1975) and Anthony J. Harding, *Coleridge and the Inspired Word* (Kingston and Montreal: McGill–Queen's University Press, 1985).

14 The question of Hegel's ultimate relationship to Christianity was a hotly disputed issue from the time of Hegel's death and continues to the present. The division of right and left Hegelians is based on whether one sees Hegel's project as using philosophy to uphold traditional Christianity (right) or as subordinating Christianity to philosophy (left). With Coleridge there is little doubt that he was attempting the former. In any case, whatever his ultimate purpose, throughout his writings Hegel took up and philosophically revitalized key Christian concepts such as the *logos* and the Incarnation. On left and right Hegelians, see William J. Brazill, *The Young Hegelians* (New Haven: Yale University Press, 1970), and Lawrence S. Stepelevich, ed., *The Young Hegelians: An Anthology* (Cambridge University Press, 1983).

15 Chytry in defending Schiller against the charge that the model of the aesthetic state inevitably subordinates the individual to the whole thus argues:

> the artwork of the state, like all artworks, contains a content specific to it which the statesman or 'Staatskünstler' overlooks to his peril: this content is the freedom of the individual human being. Creating an aesthetic state means to construct a political order consonant with this content which reinforces its further fruition into a richer, social totality. It is precisely *not* to subordinate the parts to the whole, if the whole does not promote and deepen the character of the parts. *The Aesthetic State: A Quest in Modern German Thought (Berkeley: University of California Press*, 1989), 144.

16 Albrecht Wellmer, "Reason, Utopia, and Enlightenment," in Richard J. Bernstein, ed., *Habermas and Modernity* (Cambridge, Mass.: MIT Press, 1985), 35–66, esp. 48: "the work of art becomes for Adorno the preeminent medium of a nonreified cognition and, at the same time, the paradigm for a nonrepressive integration of elements into a whole."

17 The further issue which Wellmer brings up in his critique of Adorno is that even given that Adorno's aesthetic work reconciles subjective and objective, Adorno's theory neglects the issue of communication between

human beings, intersubjective communication. I will address this issue in the final chapter.

3 SCHILLER'S AESTHETIC STATE

1. Paul de Man, *The Rhetoric of Romanticism* (New York: Columbia University Press, 1984), 265.
2. In Paul de Man's *Aesthetic Ideology* (Minneapolis: University of Minnesota Press, 1996).
3. It should be noted that de Man lifts this quote from the introduction of the English translators of the *Aesthetic Letters*, Wilkinson and Willoughby, who present it in the course of arguing *against* the tradition of connecting Schiller's aesthetic theory with the ideology of National Socialism.
4. Martha Woodmansee, *The Author, Art, and the Market: Rereading the History of Aesthetics* (New York: Columbia University Press, 1994).
5. Woodmansee, 58–9. For a critical history of this question, see Wilkinson and Willoughby's introduction to *AL*, xliii–xlviii, and Todd Curits Kontje, *Constructing Reality: A Rhetorical Analysis of Friedrich Schiller's Letters on the Aesthetic Education of Man* (New York: Peter Lang, 1987), 83–90.
6. See Woodmansee, *Author, Art*, 150, note 2.
7. "[Jeffrey] dreaded Cobbett and the popular radicals as well as Bentham and the philosophical radicals. He complained characteristically of Carlyle for being too much in earnest, and was regarded by the radicals as a mere trimmer" (*Dictionary of National Biography*, x, 709).
8. Para. 53; *Critique of Judgement*, trans. Werner S. Pluhar (Indianapolis: Hackett, 1987), 196.
9. For an extended discussion see Wilkinson and Willoughby in *AL*, 317ff.
10. This element of building a community of consensus is what Hannah Arendt, in *Lectures on Kant's Political Philosophy* (University of Chicago Press, 1982), particularly foregrounds in her analysis of the centrality of the idea of a free reading public for Kant. Arendt analyzes how Kant's idea of disinterested judgment can be seen as a process of everyone considering their own views from everyone else's point of view and then framing judgments in such a way that they could be assented to by everyone. Arendt's analysis of this process of communicability is an important predecessor to and influence on Habermas' theory of communicative action.
11. Thus Elizabeth Wilkinson and L. A. Willoughby, Schiller's English translators and commentators, argue for placing Schiller within a model of pluralistic interpretation (*AL*, 297).
12. Quoted by Friedrich Meinecke, *Cosmopolitanism and the National State*, trans. Robert B. Kimber (Princeton University Press, 1970), 46. The empire Schiller refers to is the Holy Roman Empire, by his time completely politically fragmented.
13. See Meinecke, *Cosmopolitanism and the National State*, 55–6, and Frederick C.

Beiser, *Enlightenment, Revolution, and Romanticism: The Genesis of Modern German Political Thought: 1790–1800* (Cambridge, Mass.: Harvard University Press, 1992), 229.
14 *AL*, Introduction, xlvi.

4 SYMBOL, STATE, AND CLERISY: THE AESTHETIC POLITICS OF COLERIDGE

1 The bill was passed before Coleridge could publish the work. As John Colmer notes however, "that the book appeared too late to affect the issue of Catholic Emancipation mattered little as far as the work itself was concerned, since Coleridge was more concerned with exploring fundamental ideas of Church and State than with offering specific solutions to the problem of Catholic Emancipation" (*C&S*, liv).
2 In relation to the National Church, Christianity, or the Church of Christ, is a blessed accident, a providential boon ... As the olive tree is said in its growth to fertilize the surrounding soil; to invigorate the roots of the vines in its immediate neighborhood, and to improve the strength and flavour of the wines – such is the relation of the Christian and the National Church. But as the olive is not the same plant with the vine, or with the elm or poplar (*i.e.* the State) with which the vine is wedded ... even so is Christianity, and *a fortiori* any particular scheme of Theology derived and supposed (by its partizans) to be *deduced* from Christianity ... And even so a National Church might exist, and has existed, without, because before the institution of the *Christian* Church – as the Levitical Church in the Hebrew Constitution, the Druidical in the Celtic, would suffice to prove. *C&S*, 55–6
3 In *The Rise of English Nationalism: A Cultural History, 1740–1830* (New York: St. Martin's Press, 1987), Gerald Newman puts a new interpretive twist on Burke's defense of nationalistic tradition, arguing that instead of representing the traditional ideology of the ruling class, Burke adopted it from the nationalistic groups who were in fact opposed to the French-influenced cosmopolitan ruling class. Coleridge's contrast between French political universalism and English nationalism nicely illustrates Newman's thesis. My argument here is that the adaptive tradition of the common law provides a politically conservative form of nationalism for Burke and Coleridge.
4 In book 1, chapter 1 of the *Commentaries*, Blackstone describes the major documents of the constitution as: the Magna Carta, the Petition of Right, the Bill of Rights of 1688, and the Act of Settlement. For accounts of the English state and the constitution see J. G. A. Pocock, *The Ancient Constitution and the Feudal Law. A Reissue with Retrospective* (Cambridge University Press, 1987); J. G. A. Pocock, *The Machiavellian Moment: Florentine Political Thought and the Atlantic Republican Tradition* (Princeton University Press, 1975); J. G. A. Pocock, "Burke and the Ancient Constitution," in *Politics, Language, and Time* (New York: Atheneum, 1971); and Corinne Comstock Weston, *English Constitutional Theory and the House of Lords, 1556–1832* (London: Routledge & Kegan Paul, 1965).

5   Thomas Paine, *Rights of Man* (Harmondsworth: Penguin, 1984) 71-2. Further quotations will be cited in the main text.
6   The episteme of "order" in the eighteenth century, as Michel Foucault analyzes it in *The Order of Things* (New York: Vintage, 1973), entails the construction of knowledge within the form of "mathesis," across a bounded table or grid, within which all possible positions can be charted and all possible relationships noted. Foucault analyzes these grids of representation in three areas: "the structure of beings" in natural history, "the Ars combinatoria" in general grammar, and "the value of things" in the analysis of wealth. We can add to the examples of this episteme of order, the constitution, as Paine describes it, in the area of political philosophy.
7   See Pocock, "Burke and the Ancient Constitution."
8   For an expanded discussion of the common law in relation to *Church and State*, see my "The Perfection of Reason: Coleridge and the Ancient Constitution," *Studies in Romanticism*, 32, 1993, 29–55.
9   Sir William Blackstone, *The Sovereignty of the Law: Selections from Blackstone's Commentaries on the Laws of England*, ed. Gareth Jones (University of Toronto Press, 1973), 50. Further quotations will be cited in the main text.
10 See Ben Knights, *The Idea of the Clerisy in the Nineteenth Century* (Cambridge University Press, 1978).
11 Thus while landed property is very important to Coleridge, as it ideally represents the model of national property he postulates at the origin of the state, it is only half right to assert, as Catherine Gallagher does in *The Industrial Reformation of English Fiction* (University of Chicago Press, 1985) that "Although the energy of the commercial interests is necessary to the life of the nation, the state is naturally associated with the landed interests. But Coleridge does not argue that the state represents the objective interests of agriculture; instead he argues that agriculture represents the state." (193). For, as I show, Coleridge includes in his original model of the English state the second estate of moveable wealth and its representational political institution of Parliament.
12 For a discussion of Coleridge's views on cultural elites based on the model of mystery religions, see Nigel Leask, *The Politics of Imagination in Coleridge's Critical Thought* (London: Macmillan, 1988).
13 For an overview of empirical models of representation, see Hanna Pitkin, *The Concept of Representation* (Berkeley: University of California Press, 1967).

5 THE BEST SELF AND THE PRIVATE SELF: MATTHEW ARNOLD ON CULTURE AND THE STATE

1   Chris Baldick, *The Social Mission of English Criticism, 1848–1932* (Oxford: Clarendon Press, 1983), 208.

2   Gerald Graff, "Arnold, Reason, and Common Culture," in Samuel Lipman, ed., *Culture and Anarchy* (New Haven: Yale University Press, 1995), 192.
3   "Eliot's theory of the dissociation of sensibility . . . offered a version of English literature and English social and political history in terms of mental integration, swallowing that literature and that history into 'the English mind.' In this account of history, the fusion of thought and feeling in a balanced 'sensibility' is set up as a model of mental order against which literary works and historical events are to be judged" (Baldick, *Social Mission*, 214).
4   For the relationship between these two works, see Lionel Trilling, *Matthew Arnold* (New York: Columbia University Press, 1945), 259ff.
5   This is the central thesis of Edward Alexander's *Matthew Arnold and John Stuart Mill* (New York: Columbia University Press, 1965). On these points of similarity, see also ibid., 260 and Catherine Gallagher, *The Industrial Reformation of English Fiction* (University of Chicago Press, 1985), 236.
6   Roberto Mangabeira Unger, *Knowledge and Politics* (New York: Free Press, 1975), 40. See also Sheldon S. Wolin, *Politics and Vision* (Boston: Little, Brown, 1960), 341ff.
7   John Stuart Mill, *Utilitarianism, On Liberty, and Considerations On Representative Government* (1859), edited with an introduction by H. B. Acton (London: J.M. Dent, 1972), 81.
8   See Trilling, *Matthew Arnold*, 259.
9   *The Collected Works of John Stuart Mill*, vol. 1, ed. J. Robson and J. Stillinger (University of Toronto Press, 1981), 348-9.
10 This aspect of modernism is characterized by 'the Artist in Isolation,' which Frank Kermode treats in *Romantic Image* (London: Routledge, 1957).
11 Raymond Williams, *Culture and Society, 1780-1950* (New York: Columbia University Press, 1983), 67.
12 Sheldon S. Wolin, *Politics and Vision* (Boston: Little, Brown, 1960), 349.
13 And indeed Mill is influenced by some of the same elements of German thought through his admiration of Wilhelm von Humboldt's *Spheres and Duties of Government*, which he quotes at the beginning of *On Liberty*.
14 For an account of Arnold's German influences, especially Heine, from whom the historical link to Schiller might be posited, see Joseph Carroll, *The Cultural Theory of Matthew Arnold* (Berkeley: University of California Press, 1982), 241-51.
15 In the preface to *Culture and Anarchy*, Arnold presents an extended argument about what he considers the proper conception of Christianity. He argues that it was the breadth of Christianity that originally accounted for its success, and points to its Jewish and Greek elements as evidence of the wide basis of the original Christian church. Arnold's opposition to religious Schism ('Mialism') in the preface thus reflects the overall argument of *Culture and Anarchy*.

16 See also Gallagher, *Industrial Reformation*: "Thus pure politics and culture grasp one another in a tight embrace of mutual support, having cut themselves off from any dependence on a God above or a social world below" (237).

6 AESTHETIC KINGSHIP AND QUEENSHIP: RUSKIN ON THE STATE AND THE HOME

1 For a detailed discussion of the background of typology in Ruskin, see George P. Landow, *The Aesthetic and Critical Theories of John Ruskin* (Princeton University Press, 1971), chapter 5.
2 For a comparison between's Coleridge's account of the symbol in *The Statesman's Manual* and Ruskin's theory of typology and a possible direct historical influence of the former on the latter, see Paul Sawyer, *Ruskin's Poetic Argument: The Design of the Major Works* (Ithaca and London: Cornell University Press, 1985), 94–7.
3 See *The Stones of Venice*, vol. III, (*WR*, XI, 183ff) and "The Relation of National Ethics to National Arts" (*WR*, XIX, 181).
4 For an analysis of domesticity literature, see Nancy Armstrong's *Desire and Domestic Fiction* (Oxford University Press, 1987) and Nancy Armstrong and Leonard Tennenhouse's *The Ideology of Conduct* (New York: Methuen, 1987). For a discussion of domestic ideology and Sarah Stickney Ellis in relationship to Victorian social reform, see Catherine Gallagher, *The Industrial Reformation of English Fiction* (University of Chicago Press, 1985), 119ff.
5 Sarah Stickney Ellis, *The Women of England: Their Social Duties and Domestic Habits* (New York: Appleton, 1843), 35, 36.
6 For an analysis of Ruskin's "myth-making" analysis of words, see Elizabeth K. Helsinger, *Ruskin and the Art of the Beholder* (Cambridge, Mass.: Harvard University Press, 1982), chapter 9, esp. 277–81.
7 In *Ruskin's Poetic Argument*, chapter 10, Sawyer analyzes how "Ruskin's depiction of women in general" results from the way Ruskin divides his "two ideas about virtue – that it is heroic and that it is submissive – between two separate races, men and women" (249).
8 Sawyer, *Ruskin's Poetic Argument*, describes a similar role for the ideal of the child in Ruskin's thought: "Ruskin converts his children into aesthetic objects, living artifacts that move in a kind of dance to the music of no time" (250).
9 Elizabeth Barrett Browning, *Aurora Leigh*, book 2, lines 359–62. In *Aurora Leigh and Other Poems* (London: Women's Press, 1978).
10 See Kate Millet, "The Debate over Women: Ruskin vs. Mill," in Martha Vicinus, ed., *Suffer and Be Still: Women in the Victorian Age* (Bloomington: Indiana University Press, 1973) for the classic feminist critique of Ruskin's view of women.

11 Ellis' religious views and social attitudes place her squarely in the Protestant ethic as described by Max Weber in *The Protestant Ethic and the Spirit of Capitalism*, trans. Talcott Parsons (New York: Scribner's, 1976), in which the commitment to constant work is performed ultimately not for individual personal gain, but "to increase the glory of God" (114). According to *The Dictionary of National Biography*, Ellis had been brought up a Quaker, and was married to the missionary William Ellis.

12 *The Wives of England* (London: Fisher, [1843]), [10]. We can compare a statement in a previous work, *The Daughters of England* (London: Fisher, 1842): "Thus, while the character of the daughter, the wife, and the mother, are so beautifully exemplified in connection with the dignity of a British Queen, it is the privilege of the humblest, as well as the most exalted of her subjects, to know that the heart of a woman, in all her tenderest and holiest feelings, is the same beneath the shelter of a cottage, as under the canopy of a throne," [6].

13 Bridget Hill, *Women, Work, and Sexual Politics in Eighteenth-Century England* (London: Basil Blackwell, 1989), 22.

14 Historically, the likelihood of women participating in production is strongly correlated with the household mode of production. The closer in time that a given household is to the experience of household production, the more likely it is that women will do productive work and that they will subordinate time spent in reproductive activity to that of work. During the entire nineteenth century the French economy was marked by the continuing importance of a small-scale, household organization of production. Britain, on the other hand, early developed a large-scale, factory-based system. As a result, French rates of female workforce participation were consistently higher than British rates. Louise A. Tilly and Joan W. Scott, *Women, Work, and Family* (New York: Methuen, 1987), 230.

It should be noted that Tilly and Scott are, however, critical both of stressing a sharp break between pre- and postindustrial women's labor and of assigning value judgements based on such a break.

15 This is the basis of Raymond Williams' critique of Ruskin in *Culture and Society* (New York: Columbia University Press, 1983): "The basic idea of 'organic form' produced, in Ruskin's thinking about an ideal society, the familiar notion of a paternal State. He wished to see a rigid class-structure corresponding to his ideas of 'function'... Democracy must be rejected: for its conception of the equality of men was not only untrue; it was also a disabling denial of order and 'function'" (146).

7 THE AESTHETIC AND POLITICAL SPHERES IN CONTEMPORARY THEORY: ADORNO AND HABERMAS

1 For example, this is the strain of modernism described by Frank Kermode in *Romantic Image* (London: Routledge & Kegan Paul, 1957).
2 Robert Hullot-Kentor, "Back to Adorno," *Telos*, 81, Fall 1989, 5–29, esp. 17.
3 It is Schelling, not Schiller, who is mentioned by name in *Dialectic of*

Enlightenment, and Schiller is only mentioned by name a few times in *Aesthetic Theory*.

4. *Dialectic of Enlightenment* was, of course, jointly written with Max Horkheimer. But since my purpose in referring to this book is to show the continuity with Adorno's ideas in *Aesthetic Theory*, I will simply refer to Adorno as the author when referring to *Dialectic*. For the argument that the central ideas of *Dialectic* are consistent with Adorno's writings both before and after this book, whereas there is no such continuity with Horkheimer's other works, see Hullot-Kentor, "Back to Adorno," 7–14.
5. *DE*, 186, 233–4, 245.
6. See *DE*, 189–90.
7. See Adorno's discussion of the weaving of Penelope in the *Odysseus* as an allegorical account of art in *AT*, 186–7, and Hullot-Kentor's analysis of it in "Back to Adorno," 26.
8. For an overview of these attempts, see Peter Uwe Hohendahl, *Prismatic Thought: Theodor W. Adorno* (Lincoln and London: University of Nebraska Press, 1995), 3–20.
9. See "TSR," 4, and Lambert Zuidervaart, *Adorno's Aesthetic Theory: The Redemption of Illusion* (Cambridge, Mass.: MIT Press, 1991), 111.
10. See "The Concept of Enlightenment" in *DE*.
11. For a book-length analysis, see Paul Crowther, *The Kantian Sublime: From Morality to Art* (Oxford: Clarendon Press, 1991).
12. In contrast, a later essay of Schiller's, *On the Sublime* (*Über das Erhabene*) stresses the ultimate irreconciliation between human subjectivity and nature.
13. Hullot-Kentor in his translator's introduction particularly brings out this point: "*Aesthetic Theory* is an attempt to overcome the generally recognized failing of aesthetics – its externality to its object – that Barnett Newman once did the world the favor of putting in a nutshell when he famously quipped, speaking of himself as a painter, that 'aesthetics is for me like what ornithology must be like for the birds'" (*AT*, xii).
14. Thus Adorno's aphorism: "We don't understand music, it understands us" (cited by Hullot-Kentor in his translator's introduction, *AT*, xii). Compare Wellmer's assessment of Adorno's aesthetic theory: "The light of redemption which, according to Adorno, should be cast upon reality through the medium of art, is not only not of this world, it issues... from a world that lies beyond space, time, causality, and individuation" ("TSR," 11).
15. See *PD*, 106–30, esp. 128-9.
16. The English-language versions, translated by Thomas McCarthy, are: J. Habermas, *The Theory of Communicative Action*, volume I, *Reason and the Rationalization of Society* (Boston: Beacon Press, 1984); volume II, *Lifeworld and System: A Critique of Functionalist Reason* (Boston: Beacon Press, 1987).
17. See *ICA*, 340–1, 363, 374.
18. To be completely accurate, in *The Theory of Communicative Action*, Haber-

mas distinguishes *five* types of discourse expressing validity claims: (1) theoretical discourse (cognitive-instrumental); (2) practical discourse (moral-practical) (3) aesthetic criticism; (4) therapeutic critique; and (5) explicative discourse (vol. 1, 23). But it is the first three that receive the most attention, and which correspond to Kant's three critiques of reason.

19 Hullot-Kentor, "Back to Adorno," 15.
20 The issue of the role of the aesthetic is most explicitly taken up in the discussion between Martin Jay and Habermas in *Habermas and Modernity*, ed. (Richard J. Bernstein (Cambridge, Mass.: MIT Press, 1985). Jay's chapter, "Habermas and Modernism" (125–39), analyzes Habermas' appropriation of Weber's account of the separation of validity spheres in modernity, and poses a version of the question I considered above: given this separation, how can the aesthetic sphere be reunited with the other spheres in order to deliver on its redemptive promise? In his response to Jay, Habermas gestures towards giving aesthetic experience a more central place in his system than seemed the case in *Communicative Action*, and he refers to Wellmer's work as the place in which this is worked out in detail.
21 Habermas, "Questions and Counterquestions," in Bernstein, ed., *Habermas and Modernity*, 199–203.
22 For example, in *Romanticism and Classicism*, Hulme speaks of the "avoidance of conventional language in order to get the exact curve of the thing" (in Hazard Adams, ed., *Critical Theory Since Plato* [New York: Harcourt Brace Jovanovich, 1992] 734). Similarly, Beckett's book on Proust describes the central importance of art in breaking through the deadening haze of "habit."
23 Charles Taylor, "Language and Society," in Axel Honneth and Hans Joas, eds., *Communicative Action: Essays on Jürgen Habermas's "The Theory of Communicative Action"* (Cambridge, Mass.: MIT Press, 1991), 24.
24 These appear as chapters 6 and 7 of Habermas' *Postmetaphysical Thinking: Philosophical Essays*, trans. William Mark Hohengarten (Cambridge, Mass.: MIT Press, 1992).

Index

Because the four central aesthetic statists, Schiller, Coleridge, Arnold, and Ruskin, are so often mentioned (and mentioned together) in this book, this name/work index only lists citations for their specific works.

Abrams, M. H. 12, 13, 78, 138 n2
Addison, Joseph 123
Adorno, Theodor 5, 30, 34–8, 112–22, 124–5, 128–9
   Aesthetic Theory 113, 115, 121, 125
   Dialectic of Enlightenment 16, 34–5, 43, 113–15, 122
Alexander, Edward 147 n5
Alison, Archibald 46
Arendt, Hannah 23, 140 n23, 144 n10
   Lectures on Kant's Political Philosophy 23, 24
Aristotle 118
   Poetics 119
Armstrong, Nancy 148 n4
Arnold, Matthew
   Culture and Anarchy 3, 23, 82–90, 102
   "Democracy" 76–7, 81–2
   "The Study of Poetry" 87–91

Babbitt, Irving 18
Baldick, Chris 74–5, 86, 146 n1, 147 n3
Barfield, Owen 142 n7, n9
Beckett, Samuel 129, 151 n22
Beiser, Frederick C. 21, 138 n7, 141 n24
Benjamin, Walter 28, 35, 141 n2
Bentham, Jeremy 19, 26, 78
Bernstein, Richard J. 151 n20
Blackstone, William 62, 65–6
Brazill, William J. 143 n14
Brooks, Cleanth 141 n1
Browning, Elizabeth Barrett
   Aurora Leigh 107
Burke, Edmund 61–6
Bürger, Gottfried August 41
Butler, Marilyn 13, 138 n7
Byron, George Gordon 140 n21

Carlyle, Thomas 144 n7
Carroll, Joseph 147 n13
Chandler, James 138 n7
Chytry, Josef 5–7, 138 nn8–9, 139 n8, 141 n27, 143 n15
Cobbett, William 144 n7
Coleridge, Samuel Taylor
   Constitution of Church and State 12, 17, 59–73, 81
   The Friend 12, 59, 61
   The Statesman's Manual 3, 30–6, 59, 89
Colley, Linda 21, 140 n20
Colmer, John 67–8, 145 n1
Cowling, Maurice 137 n6
Crowther, Paul 150 n11

De Man, Paul 3, 8, 12, 39, 40
   "The Rhetoric of Temporality." 13, 33, 137 n5

Eliot, Thomas Stearns 74–6
Ellis, Sarah Stickney 104, 108–9
Fichte, Immanuel Hermann 45
Foucault, Michel 146 n6
Frei, Hans W. 143 n11

Gallagher, Catherine 146 n11, 147 n5, 148 n4, n16
Graff, Gerald 75, 86, 137 n6, 147 n2

Habermas, Jürgen 5, 9, 10, 17, 30, 41–3, 112, 121–36
   Philosophical Discourse of Modernity 15, 122, 125, 127
   Structural Transformation of the Public Sphere 43, 123–4, 132, 135

The Theory of Communicative Action 125–7, 131
"Individuation Through Socialization" 134–5
"The Unity of Reason in the Diversity of its Voices" 134
Harding, Anthony J. 143 n13
Hartman, Geoffrey 12, 138 n4
Hegel, Georg Wilhelm Friedrich 1, 6, 7, 14–7, 30–3, 109, 113, 120, 134, 141 n5, 143 n14
  Phenomenology of Spirit 12, 15, 33
  Philosophy of Right 7, 16, 142 n8
Heidegger, Martin 6
Helsinger, Elizabeth K. 148 n6
Herder, Johann Gottfried 41, 134
Hill, Bridget 109, 149 n13
Hobbes, Thomas 22
Hohendahl, Peter Uwe 150 n8
Hölderlin, Friedrich 6, 15, 32
Horkheimer, Max 16, 150 n4
Hullot-Kentor, David 113, 127, 149 n2, 150 n4, n7, n13
Hulme, Thomas Ernest 18, 129
  Romanticism and Classicism 151 n22
Humboldt, Wilhelm von 147 n13

Jay, Martin 151 n20
Jeffrey, Francis 46–7

Kaiser, David A. 143 n13, 146 n8
Kant, Immanuel 14–15, 22–4, 31, 39, 44–5, 48–53, 58, 72, 85–6, 107, 110, 113, 120, 125–6
  Critique of Judgement 40, 48, 119
  Idea for a Universal History with a Cosmopolitan Purpose 141 n24
  Perpetual Peace 23
Kedourie, Elie 20, 139 n10, nn13–14, 140 n17
Kermode, Frank 147 n10, 149 n1
Knapp, Steven 137 n5
Knights, Ben 146 n10
Kontje, Todd Curits 144 n5

Laclau, Ernesto 2, 137 n3
Landow, George P. 95, 148 n1
Lask, Emil 125
Leask, Nigel 138 n7, 146 n12
Leavis, F. R. 74–6
Lentricchia, Frank 141 n3
Levinson, Marjorie 138 n7
Lipman, Samuel 137 n6
Liu, Alan 138 n.7
Lloyd, David 137 n4
Locke, John 22, 64, 71

Lukács, Georg
  The Young Hegel 141 n28

McFarland, Thomas 142 n10
McGann, Jerome 1, 137 n1, 138 n7
Mandeville, Bernard 23
Marcus, Steven 137 n6
Marcuse, Herbert 6
Marx, Karl 6, 8, 14, 16
  Critique of Hegel's Philosophy of Right 16
Meinecke, Friedrich 139–40 n15
Mill, James 19
Mill, John Stuart 14, 26, 72–3, 76–81, 90, 112, 139 n12
  Considerations on Representative Government 19, 23, 77, 79–81, 86
  On Liberty 26, 76–8, 85–6
Millet, Kate 148 n10
Milton, John 71, 102–3
Moritz, Karl Philipp 40–2
Morris, William 96
Mouffe, Chantal 2, 137 n3
Müller, Adam 140 n16

Newman, Gerald 21, 140 nn20–1, 145 n3
Nietzsche, Friedrich 6
Novalis 21, 25

Orsini, G. N. G. 142 n6

Paine, Thomas 62–4
Pater, Walter 111
Patmore, Coventry 104
Pinchbeck, Ivy 109
Pippin, Robert 141–2 n5
Pitkin, Hanna 146 n13
Plato 30–1
  Republic 25
Pocock, J. G. A. 64, 140 n19, 145 n4
Proust, Marcel 129, 151 n22

Richards, I. A. 131
Richardson, Samuel 123
Rorty, Richard 1, 26, 137 n2, 141 n29
Ruskin, John
  Modern Painters, volume two 92, 93–5, 98, 106
  Sesame and Lilies 92–4, 97, 100–2, 107, 110
  The Stones of Venice 92–3, 95
  The Two Paths 93, 97
  Unto this Last 92–3, 100, 102
  "The Deteriorative Power of Conventional Art Over Nations" 98
  "The Nature of Gothic" 93, 95–7, 99, 109
  "Of King's Treasuries" 100–3

Ruskin, John (*cont.*)
  "Of Queens' Gardens"   103–7
  "The Relation of National Ethics to
    National Arts"   98–100

Saussure, Ferdinand de   133
Sawyer, Paul   148 n2, nn7–8
Schelling, Friedrich Wilhelm Joseph von   6,
    15, 32, 149 n3
Schiller, Friedrich
  Aesthetic Letters   1, 2, 17, 36, 39–58, 69, 81,
    86, 91, 97, 113, 119, 125
  On the Sublime   150 n12
Schlegel, Friedrich von   21, 25, 32
Schulze, Hagen   140 n18
Scott, Joan W.   109, 149 n14
Shaffer, Elinor S.   143 n13
Sidney, Sir Philip   71
Simpson, David   138 n7, 139 n7
Stepelevich, Lawrence S.   143 n14
Spenser, Edmund   71

Taylor, Charles   133–4, 151 n23
Tilly, Louise A.   109, 149 n14
Trilling, Lionel   147 n4, n8

Unger, Roberto Mangabeira   76–7, 147 n6

Wagner, Richard   6
Weber, Max   14, 16, 125–6
  The Protestant Ethic and the Spirit of Capitalism
    149 n11
Wellmer, Albrecht   36, 38, 113, 119–21,
    127–31, 143 nn16–17, 150 n14
Weston, Corinne Comstock   140 n19
Wilkinson, Elizabeth   55, 144 n3, n5, n9, n11
Wilkinson, James H.   141–2 n3
Williams, Raymond   3, 13–14, 24, 111
  Culture and Society   5–6, 11–12, 78, 91, 137 n4,
    149 n15
Willoughby, L. A.   55, 144 n3, n5, n9, n11
Winckelmann, Johann Joachim   6
Wolin, Sheldon   79, 147 n6, n12
Woodmansee, Martha   40–3, 46, 48, 111,
    144 n4
Woodring, Carl   18, 139 n9
Wordsworth, William   21
  Excursion   12
  The Prelude   12

Zuidervaart, Lambert   150 n9

CAMBRIDGE STUDIES IN ROMANTICISM

GENERAL EDITORS
MARILYN BUTLER, *University of Oxford*
JAMES CHANDLER, *University of Chicago*

1. *Romantic Correspondence: Women, Politics and the Fiction of Letters*
   MARY A. FAVRET

2. *British Romantic Writers and the East: Anxieties of Empire*
   NIGEL LEASK

3. *Edmund Burke's Aesthetic Ideology*
   Language, Gender and Political Economy in Revolution
   TOM FURNISS

4. *Poetry as an Occupation and an Art in Britain, 1760–1830*
   PETER MURPHY

5. *In the Theatre of Romanticism: Coleridge, Nationalism, Women*
   JULIE A. CARSON

6. *Keats, Narrative and Audience*
   ANDREW BENNETT

7. *Romance and Revolution: Shelley and the Politics of a Genre*
   DAVID DUFF

8. *Literature, Education and Romanticism*
   Reading as Social Practice, 1780–1832
   ALAN RICHARDSON

9. *Women Writing about Money: Women's Fiction in England, 1790–1820*
   EDWARD COPELAND

10. *Shelley and the Revolution in Taste: The Body and the Natural World*
    TIMOTHY MORTON

11. *William Cobbett: The Politics of Style*
    LEONORA NATTRASS

12. *The Rise of Supernatural Fiction, 1762–1800*
   E. J. CLERY

13. *Women Travel Writers and the Language of Aesthetics, 1716–1818*
   ELIZABETH A. BOHLS

14. *Napoleon and English Romanticism*
   SIMON BAINBRIDGE

15. *Romantic Vagrancy: Wordsworth and the Simulation of Freedom*
   CELESTE LANGAN

16. *Wordsworth and the Geologists*
   JOHN WYATT

17. *Wordsworth's Pope: A Study in Literary Historiography*
   ROBERT J. GRIFFIN

18. *The Politics of Sensibility*
   Race, Gender and Commerce in the Sentimental Novel
   MARKMAN ELLIS

19. *Reading Daughters' Fictions, 1709–1834*
   Novels and Society from Manley to Edgeworth
   CAROLINE GONDA

20. *Romantic Identities: Varieties of Subjectivity, 1774–1830*
   ANDREA K. HENDERSON

21. *Print Politics*
   The Press and Radical Opposition in Early Nineteenth-Century England
   KEVIN GILMARTIN

22. *Reinventing Allegory*
   THERESA M. KELLEY

23. *British Satire and the Politics of Style, 1789–1832*
   GARY DYER

24. *The Romantic Reformation*
Religious Politics in English Literature, 1789–1824
ROBERT M. RYAN

25. *De Quincey's Romanticism*
Canonical Minority and the Forms of Transmission
MARGARET RUSSETT

26. *Coleridge on Dreaming*
Romanticism, Dreams and the Medical Imagination
JENNIFER FORD

27. *Romantic Imperialism*
Universal Empire and the Culture of Modernity
SAREE MAKDISI

28. *Ideology and Utopia in the Poetry of William Blake*
NICHOLAS M. WILLIAMS

29. *Sexual Politics and the Romantic Author*
SONIA HOFKOSH

30. *Lyric and Labour in the Romantic Tradition*
ANNE JANOWITZ

31. *Poetry and Politics in the Cockney School*
Keats, Shelley, Hunt and their Circle
JEFFREY N. COX

32. *Rousseau, Robespierre and English Romanticism*
GREGORY DART

33. *Contesting the Gothic Fiction*
Genre and Cultural Conflict, 1764–1832
JAMES WATT

34. *Romanticism, Aesthetics, and Nationalism*
DAVID ARAM KAISER